The Next American Revolution

The publisher gratefully acknowledges the generous support of the African American Studies Endowment Fund of the University of California Press Foundation.

The Next American Revolution

Sustainable Activism
for the Twenty-First Century
Updated and Expanded Edition

Grace Lee Boggs

With Scott Kurashige
Foreword by Danny Glover
New Afterword with Immanuel Wallerstein

UNIVERSITY OF CALIFORNIA PRESS
Berkeley   Los Angeles   London

University of California Press, one of the most distinguished university presses in the United States, enriches lives around the world by advancing scholarship in the humanities, social sciences, and natural sciences. Its activities are supported by the UC Press Foundation and by philanthropic contributions from individuals and institutions. For more information, visit www.ucpress.edu.

University of California Press
Berkeley and Los Angeles, California

University of California Press, Ltd.
London, England

© 2011, 2012 by The Regents of the University of California

First paperback printing 2012

Library of Congress Cataloging-in-Publication Data

Boggs, Grace Lee.
  The next American revolution : sustainable activism for the twenty-first century / Grace Lee Boggs with Scott Kurashige ; foreword by Danny Glover.
    p.   cm.
  Includes bibliographical references and index.
  ISBN 978-0-520-27259-0 (paper : alk. paper)
    1. Social action—United States—History—21st century.   2. Social movements—United States—History—21st century.   3. Sustainable development—United States—History—21st century.   I. Kurashige, Scott. II. Title.
  HN65.B634   2011
  303.48′4097309051—dc22   2010039659

Manufactured in the United States of America

20 19 18 17
10   9   8   7   6

To Jimmy Boggs, who thought and acted dialectically

CONTENTS

FOREWORD

DANNY GLOVER

This book is about our journey. It is drawn from Grace's reflections on her journey, but it is about our journey as well.

When Grace Lee Boggs celebrated her ninety-fourth birthday in the summer of 2009, I knew it was important for me to be there in Detroit with her and those who love her. Ossie Davis, a close friend of Grace and Jimmy Boggs, often said that he went to places where he was invited to speak because he knew that was where he was supposed to be at that moment.

As I traveled outside the United States for seven weeks, I thought repeatedly about coming to Grace's party. It seemed that every single thing that happened to me in that period of time brought me in close connection to what was going on in Detroit.

In Rwanda I stood at the memorial to genocide among the remains of more than three hundred thousand people buried in a place where you cannot imagine three hundred thousand people even being able to stand. And standing there, I was moved nation and to support the Mubaraks of the world but for constructive human and domestic needs.

We must see the floods and mudslides ravaging the Midwest and those that have killed scores of people in Pakistan and China as a challenge to stem the catastrophic effects of global warming, the product of a consumerist desire for boundless economic growth infecting both the 1 percent and the middle class.

The ongoing struggles, from Wisconsin to the Occupy/Decolonize movement, can become a beacon of the next American Revolution if those involved in the struggle recognize that our current crises are rooted in the decline of the empire, which made possible both the middle-class standard of living and the welfare state, with its thousands of public employees to take care of tasks for which we the people must become increasingly responsible.

With the end of empire, we are coming to an end of the epoch of *rights*. We have entered the epoch of *responsibilities*, which requires new, more socially-minded human beings and new, more participatory and place-based concepts of citizenship and democracy.

FROM DISAPPEARING JOBS
TO REIMAGINING WORK

As millions of Americans struggle to make ends meet and another election cycle approaches, voters are demanding more jobs, and politicians are yet again promising to create them. In cities like Detroit, we know we need a new approach. Abandoned by global corporations, community people are struggling to build more self-reliant, localized economies, growing our own food, and restoring the neighbor to the 'hood.

At the peak of the industrial epoch in the twentieth century we were convinced that progress depended on the continuing expansion of government and mammoth enterprises like General Motors. It was difficult to remember that "doing it for yourself" is probably one of the three or four key instincts that we have inherited through evolution over millions of years. It is part of what makes us human. If we can do something for ourselves, we don't feel as powerless as the person who has to get somebody else to do it for them. The more we can do for ourselves, the more in control of our future we are.

This is an idea whose time has come back as we enter the postindustrial epoch. I have been so inspired by the Detroiters who in the midst of our city's devastation are discovering new ways to make Detroit a City of Hope. We are seeking to expand our humanity not by growing our economy but by growing our souls.

Those of us who live here feel fortunate. Our city has a proud tradition of plowing new ground. We are excited to be doing so now—literally in our urban farms and gardens and figuratively in our nonstop conversation about a new economy.

Industrial jobs came here early and in large numbers. They left here early and in large numbers.

We know that our current political system cannot fulfill our need for meaningful work. In the Black Power movement of the 1960s, we struggled for and won "community control" of schools. Now our public school system has been hijacked by state-appointed emergency financial managers, whose primary tasks have been closing schools, privatizing services, and laying off employees.

We struggled for Black political power and stood in solidarity with all the civil rights activists who sacrificed and died for the right to vote. Now, with analysts concluding that even the drastic wage cuts and layoffs of city workers proposed by local officials are inadequate to stave off insolvency, the State of Michigan has way out of no way" demonstrate how the vacant lot represents the possibilities of cultural revolution.

Detroit's cultural revolution is transforming how we view ourselves, our surroundings, and our institutions. We are making a life and not just a living, by feeding ourselves, educating our children, and taking more responsibility for each other and our communities.

This cultural revolution is very different from the cultural revolution involving the education of mostly illiterate Russian peasants advocated by Lenin after the Bolshevik seizure of state power in 1917. It is also very different from Mao's 1966 cultural revolution, which sent millions of educated Chinese youth to work in the countryside and learn from the peasantry. It goes beyond the cultural revolution of the 1960s that began to redefine race, gender, and generational relations.

Today's cultural revolution, which is emerging from the ground up especially in Detroit, is as awesome as the transitions from hunting and gathering to agriculture eleven thousand years ago and from agriculture to industry a few hundred years ago.

Because in different ways we are all in the midst of this epochal shift, we all need to practice visionary organizing. I anticipate that in the second decade of the twenty-first century we will deepen and broaden the visionary advances that became visible in the first decade.

It will become clearer to more millions that our good health depends on our making the good food revolution. Instead of relying on an industrialized food system that keeps us ignorant and powerless about what we take into our bodies, we will be producing most of our food locally, not only growing vegetables on neighboring lots, rooftops, and balconies but also raising chickens in backyard coops and fish in local and home aquariums. This is not just a question of physical health but also one of spiritual values.

In the second decade of the twenty-first century, I anticipate that our work will increasingly take the form of crafts. As robots replaced human beings on the production line in the twentieth century, we began to realize that, while the industrial age produced material abundance, it was really a digression in the continuing evolution of the human race: the labor which it required, be our payment high or low, was so fragmenting and inhuman that it could be done by robots.

In this decade I anticipate that in view of the obvious failures of No Child Left Behind and Race to the Top, the continuing schools crisis will be resolved by our creating community- and place-based schools. By making the tackling and solving of community problems a normal and natural part of the school curriculum from K-12, our schools will empower children and young people, showing our respect for them as fellow citizens. We will finally realize that the best way to interest children and young people in their own education is by community involvement and not by tests, threats, and other punitive measures.

In these desperate times, we must come together as inventors and discoverers committed to creating ideas and practice, vision and projects to help heal civilization.

As I approach my ninety-seventh birthday with seven decades of movement activism behind me, I remain filled with hope that a better future is within our grasp. My ongoing work in Detroit and encounters with people from all over the world engaged in visionary organizing continue to provide me with assurance that we have the power within ourselves to create the world anew.

And for that I am blessed.

Detroit, Michigan, 2011

Charles and Sandra Simmons, Lottie Spady, and Ilana Weaver are among the authors' and the center's many friends in Detroit who contributed to activities related to this book. The Boggs Center will receive all the authors' royalties from this book.

Special thanks to Danny Glover, whose generous and moving foreword grew out of many hours of dialogue with Grace in her home.

The University of Michigan has been a critical site for the development and circulation of ideas in this book. Scott would especially like to recognize the faculty, staff, and students of the Program in American Culture, Department of History, and Asian/Pacific Islander American Studies Program. We also thank President Mary Sue Coleman; the Center for Afroamerican and African Studies; Office of Academic Multicultural Initiatives; Rev. Dr. Martin Luther King Jr. Symposium; University Housing's Office of Cultural Awareness and Diversity Education; Baits Multicultural Council; Global Intercultural Experience for Undergraduates Program; Residential College; Semester in Detroit; Arts of Citizenship; Ginsberg Center; Department of Women's Studies; School of Social Work; School of Education; and the International Institute.

Research and writing of this book were supported by Harvard University's Charles Warren Center for Studies in American History, where Scott was a fellow during 2008–9. Special thanks to the faculty coordinators, Evelyn Brooks Higginbotham and Ken Mack; center director, Joyce Chaplin; and administrative staff, Arthur Patton-Hock and Larissa Kennedy; as well as the amazing group of fellow colleagues in residence who commented on a presentation of material related to this book.

Many of the issues and themes presented in this book first appeared in Grace's weekly columns for the *Michigan Citizen*, metro Detroit's leading publication documenting the struggles of grassroots activists and urban residents. Special thanks are owed to the Kelly family.

Monthly Review Press has been a steadfast and ardent supporter of Jimmy and Grace for five decades. Some ideas and passages from this book were originally published in the new introduction by Grace Lee Boggs for the reissue of James and Grace Lee Boggs, *Revolution and Evolution in the Twentieth Century,* vii-xlvi (copyright 1974 and 2008 by Monthly Review Press and reprinted by permission of the Monthly Review Foundation). Thanks to Martin Paddio.

Many others helped to advance recognition of our work or played a role in the dozens of speeches, articles, and interviews that served as preliminary testing grounds for the ideas in this book. The long list of organizations, publications, and projects we wish to thank includes but is not limited to the Allied Media Conference, American Educational Research Association, Animating Democracy (a program of Americans for the Arts), Asian Americans United, Association for Asian American Studies, Barnard College, Beloved Communities Initiative, *Bill Moyers Journal,* Boggs Educational Center, Bryn Mawr College, Cass Corridor Neighborhood Development Corporation, Catherine Ferguson Academy, Central United Methodist Church, *Chicken-Bones,* CUNY Graduate Center *Advocate, Democracy Now!,* Detroit Agricultural Network, Detroit Asian Youth Project, Detroit City Council, *Detroit Free Press, Detroit News,* Detroit Summer, *Detroit Today/The Craig Fahle Show,* Earthworks Garden–Capuchin Soup Kitchen, *Fault Lines, First of the Month,* First Unitarian Universalist Church of Detroit, flypmedia, *Garden Stories,* Genesis Lutheran Church, *The Grace Lee Project,* Harvard University's Department of African and African American Studies and

INTRODUCTION

SCOTT KURASHIGE

These are perilous times, shaped by economic meltdown, wars, persistent social divisions, and the prospect of environmental calamities for whose full extent few are remotely prepared. A view of the modern world driven by American dominance, cheap oil, easy credit, and conspicuous consumption is rapidly unraveling before our eyes. In the face of such crises, the institutions of the status quo appear increasingly outmoded and ineffective.

Because the future is more uncertain than ever, these perilous times are also precious times. Collectively, we have a window of opportunity to rediscover the nonmaterial things that bring us joy and fulfillment. I have learned to savor every minute of time with my four-year-old daughter not only because I know how quickly children grow up but also because I have no idea what state the world will be in when she is my age. Will it be a world torn apart by famines, pandemics, and wars over vanishing supplies of oil and freshwater? Will crises for humanity prompt a resurgence of racism, patriarchy, jingoism, authoritarianism, or other forms of dehumanization we once thought anathema to a modern sensibility?

Time is most precious, however, because we can still act to avert the worst consequences of human-induced catastrophe in the twenty-first century. As terrible as the walls crumbling around us look and feel, we must avoid falling into total dismay. And we can rest assured that the challenges of the new millennium will prompt a great deal of soul searching and unforeseeable expressions of love and creativity.

It is in contradictory times like these—the best and worst of times—that the voice of a movement elder like Grace Lee Boggs proves invaluable. Here is a voice that can help guide us to the next stage, one in which we move from reacting to crisis to creating alternative modes of work, politics, and human interaction that will collectively forge the next American Revolution.

AN UNLIKELY JOURNEY

Few of us will be lucky to live to ninety-five years of age with our faculties, let alone the full and vigorous abilities with which Grace Lee Boggs continues to approach her political and intellectual life. Indeed, for many of the youth she regularly encounters, Grace must come across as older than history itself. She entered this world during the tumult of the Great War (before humankind knew it would be the *First* World War), a time when Jim Crow was the law of the land, the cars and planes that would define twentieth-century life were still novelties, and electrical appliances were at best household luxuries. Grace was born two years before John F. Kennedy and ten years before Malcolm X. When she was completing her PhD, Martin Luther King Jr. was still in grade school. Is there any other figure in the United States today who can reflect on seven decades of activist life and history with the vibrancy of Grace Lee Boggs?

As James Boggs (1919–93)—Grace's life partner, intellectual collaborator, and political comrade for forty years—was wont to say, "Just coming out of your mother's womb does not make you a human being."[1] Jimmy Boggs urged us to recognize the role creative thinking and responsible action play in advancing humanity. To understand what Grace represents to us today, we might add, "Just getting old doesn't make you wise."

Grace's political and humanitarian vision draws from both a rich lifetime of experience in struggle and a rigorous commitment to critical thinking. It emanates from the meeting ground of continuity and change: the wisdom to highlight the vital components of our history, culture, and tradition that have sustained community across countless human generations, combined with the radical spirit to think and act anew, rise to new challenges, and overcome that which is discordant and malignant in society.

Her vision and practice are also the product of a most unlikely journey, one in which she has consciously grounded herself within a tight-knit community while opening herself up to influences from diverse and varied sources of inspiration. We need to appreciate how the personal and political identifications that consigned Grace to the margins of twentieth-century politics and scholarship now uniquely position her to speak to the dilemmas of twenty-first-century America.

Grace began to leave her mark on the world in 1940, when she completed a PhD in philosophy from Bryn Mawr College—an unprecedented achievement for a U.S.-born daughter of Chinese immigrants. But finding no home in an academic order still dominated by the old white boys' network, she soon took to the streets, landing on the South Side of Chicago near the end of the Great Depression, just as the African American communities of the urban North were awakening to their collective political power. Grace had discovered her mission in life: to be a movement activist.

As she recounts in these pages, Grace had the great fortune to be not just a witness to but also an active participant in the humanity-stretching movements of the twentieth century, including the civil rights movement, labor movement, women's movement, Black Power movement, Asian American movement, and environmental justice movement. During her seven decades of struggle, her close associates have included people who changed the course of history, such as the legendary actors Ruby Dee and Ossie Davis, the Pan-Africanist and Ghanaian president Kwame Nkrumah, and the pioneering black Marxist C. L. R. James. Grace once met with Malcolm X to propose that he join the revolutionary organizing activities she was undertaking with other Black Power activists in Detroit.[2]

Still, the most formidable figure in her life has undoubtedly been Jimmy Boggs. An autoworker and autodidact from the Deep South, Jimmy was born in the age of sharecropping and joined the Great Migration to the industrial North. There he lived to see the devastating effects of automation, deindustrialization, and capital flight on the labor movement, the black proletariat, and the Motor City that became his adopted hometown. The consummate organic intellectual, Jimmy Boggs drew insights from his personal experience through three great epochs (agriculture, industry, and automation). But he also sought new modes of understanding from book knowledge to tackle unsolved problems, always working to make his radical ideas accessible and persuasive to the people in the community surrounding him. Jimmy possessed a unique ability to both appreciate and transcend Grace Lee's world shaped by university philosophers, left-wing polemicists, and radical agitators. Just a couple of months after she moved to Detroit in June 1953, they became engaged. Grace would later remark that her partnership with Jimmy helped to make her a whole person.

If it is possible to pinpoint one characteristic that distinguishes Grace, it is that she embodies the unity of theory and practice in a manner that has become increasingly rare. In the United States we have a disturbing tendency to reduce the production of ideas and knowledge to academics. Americans go to school for a finite period of time to "learn things," then they go out into the "real world" to put what they have learned into practice. Many U.S. activists are too quick to view intellectual work as the domain of those with academic jobs, deeming it elitist in general, and too prone to discount the role creative thinking plays in movement building. To this brand of activist, signs of inequality and injustice seem obvious, as does protesting the status quo and demanding the redistribution of resources and power.

By contrast, Grace has continued to devote much of her time to study and reflection even as she parted ways with the academic world for a life of organizing. Reflecting her belief in "the power of ideas," books and publications can be found stacked from floor to ceiling in every room of her modest flat, and over the past decade she has spent an increasing amount of time surfing the best writings and videos on the Web. Unlike those radicals devoted almost exclusively to action in pursuit of an "old truth" they discovered during their political awakening, Grace is constantly seeking to make sense of new developments and conditions, tracking changes both within the dominant culture and the forces of resistance.

This behavior is consistent with her imperative to "think dialectically"—a maxim drawn from her study of the philosopher G. W. F. Hegel. Because reality is constantly changing, we must constantly detect and analyze the emerging contradictions that are driving this change. And if reality is changing around us, we cannot expect good ideas to hatch within an ivory tower. They instead emerge and develop through daily life and struggle, through collective study and debate among diverse entities, and through trial and error within multiple contexts.

Grace often attributes her "having been born female and Chinese" to her sense of being an outsider to mainstream society. Over the past decade she has sharpened this analysis considerably. Reflecting on the limits of her prior encounters with radicalism, Grace fully embraces the feminist critique not only of gender discrimination and inequality but also of the masculinist tendencies that too often come to define a certain brand of movement organizing—one driven by militant posturing, a charismatic form of hierarchical leadership, and a static notion of power seen as a scarce commodity to be acquired and possessed.

Grace has struck up a whole new dialogue and built relationships with Asian American activists and intellectuals since the 1998 release of her autobiography, *Living for Change*. Her reflections on these encounters have reinforced her repeated observation that marginalization serves as a form of liberation. Thus, she has come away impressed with the particular ability of movement-oriented Asian Americans to dissect U.S. society in new ways that transcend the mind-sets of blacks and whites, to draw on their transnational experiences to rethink the nature of the global order, and to enact new propositions free of the constraints and baggage weighing down those embedded in the status quo.

Still, Grace's practical connection to a constantly changing reality for most of her adult life has stemmed from an intimate relationship with the African American community—so much so that informants from the Cointelpro days surmised she was probably Afro-Chinese.[3] This connection to black America (and to a lesser degree the pan-African world) has made her a source of intrigue for younger generations grappling with the rising complexities of race and diversity. It has been sustained through both political commitments and personal relationships. Living in Detroit for more than a half century, Grace has developed a stature as one of Motown's most cherished citizens: penning a weekly column for the city's largest-circulation black community newspaper; regularly profiled in the mainstream and independent media; frequently receiving awards and honors through no solicitation of her own; constantly visited by students, intellectuals, and activists from around the world; and even speaking on behalf of her friend Rosa Parks after the civil rights icon became too frail for public appearances.

But though Grace has been associated with historical figures and has dined with luminaries on more than one occasion, her daily activities are primarily occupied by meetings and communications with people working at a grassroots level to transform blocks, neighborhoods, and cities. These new and renewing relationships with people and ideas particularly feed Grace's creative spirit and nourish her soul, for every narrative—of individuals or movements shared face-to-face, by e-mail, or through written publications—brings with it new lessons in life and struggle, new reasons to believe that humankind can achieve that which still must be accomplished. Be they artists or statesmen, shopkeepers or grandparents, elders are rightfully concerned with their legacy. Grace, however, still bristles with the energy of a twenty-five-year-old movement activist, and this is readily apparent to everyone who crosses her path. As a result, this book draws lessons and meaning from the past, but it is clearly focused on the present and future.

And this is where my role in this project—both the writing of this book and its existence as a living document to be discussed and debated after publication—begins to take shape as a collaborator. I first met Grace in 1998, shortly after reading her autobiography, while a graduate student at UCLA. On the advice of the veteran organizer and professor Glenn Omatsu, I invited her to speak at an Asian American activism conference I had organized. Since 2000 I have worked as a professor of history and ethnic studies at the University of Michigan, located forty miles west of Detroit in Ann Arbor. In this sense my life trajectory departs from Grace's path. Although we are both American-born Asians, I am a product and beneficiary of the movements to democratize and diversify higher education.

At the most basic level, I have approached this project as a scholarly editor working to shape Grace's articles, columns, speeches, notes, and correspondence into coherent chapters. After moving to Detroit a decade ago, I began to interview her extensively and comb through the stacks and stacks of boxes holding a treasure trove of historical documents dating back to the 1940s. But I was quickly awed by how extraordinarily productive she remained as an intellectual—reading a half-dozen books per week while keeping tabs on a wide range of periodicals. Correspondingly, her weekly newspaper columns, e-mail missives, and frequent lectures bristled with insights that brought historical bearing on contemporary problems. I took it upon myself to keep an ongoing archive of these papers as well. Subsequently, I proposed to her that we work in tandem to reshape these materials into this book. Just as my initial encounter with Grace has turned into a protracted effort to reconstruct society from the ground up, my initial plan to gather a collection of Grace's various writings for publication turned into a protracted effort to construct a freestanding manuscript from the ground up.

At another level I see my role as that of intergenerational translator. Born at the height of the Vietnam War era and inhabiting a world transformed by it, I have through academic research and interpersonal dialogue devoted more time than most others my age to making sense of the sixties. At the same time, my professional and community-based work has continuously challenged me to understand and communicate with high school and college-aged youth, whose ability to connect with the past has been severely compromised by a post-MTV culture that reduces history to symbolism and iconography.

For much of the past decade, I lived in Detroit, about five minutes away from Grace's Eastside home, while undertaking various community activist projects and serving as a board member of the James and Grace Lee Boggs Center to Nurture Community Leadership—an organization founded by friends of Jimmy and Grace in the aftermath of Jimmy's passing to carry on the development of ideas and actions consistent with their radical spirit. I moved to Detroit because I felt, just as Grace did in the 1950s, that making a connection to the movement-building activities going on in Motown was somehow crucial to my development as an intellectual and activist. Generally speaking, as Grace would say, I needed to become more whole as a human being. Now I see my task as seeking out those who want and need to come along and further this unlikely journey.

REIMAGINING THE AMERICAN DREAM
IN DETROIT

While only one chapter in this book focuses specifically on Detroit, it must be stated that the whole of this book has been molded by the city.[4] Once hailed as the place that gave birth to the American Dream, Detroit has since been lambasted, ridiculed, and left to rot as the site of its demise. But as we wrestle with the unresolved contradictions of the industrial age and confront the new contradictions of postindustrial society, the current economic and environmental crises help us to appreciate how Detroit's fate is not exceptional but paradigmatic. Above all, Detroit is the place that has crystallized for us Martin Luther King Jr.'s call for a "revolution of values" against the "giant triplets of racism, militarism and materialism."

Detroit brings into clear focus the relationship between the American Dream and MLK's giant triplets. It was twentieth-century Detroit's advanced technology and models of organized production—embodied by the Fordist assembly line depicted in Diego Rivera's epic *Detroit Industry* mural—that made the Motor City one of the world's great centers of wealth creation. Though he scorned the appropriation of labor power and maldistribution of wealth, the Marxist Rivera reveals through this mural how he shared with the captains of industry an unflinching belief in progress.

Even the Great Depression, although it severely curtailed corporate profits and sent stock shares plummeting, did not immediately overturn the vulgar materialist mind-set. It took the organization of the industrial union movement—one of the greatest and most influential social movements in history—to shake the foundations of the social order. The rights and benefits that both union and nonunion workers have enjoyed over the past seven decades are due in no small measure to the courageous and imaginative actions of Michigan autoworkers and their community allies—from the martyrs of the 1932 massacre outside the titanic Ford Rouge plant in Dearborn to the heroes of the 1936–37 sit-down strike at the GM/Fisher plant in Flint. Threatened with a shutdown at the point of production, the Big 3 automakers would learn to respect the rights of their workers. Then both labor and management would join forces to build the engines propelling U.S. victories in World War II as Detroit became the nation's "arsenal of democracy."

Out of this age of movement building emerged the grand vision of social democracy. Grace considers herself fortunate to have first learned how to think from social democratic intellectuals such as John Dewey and George Herbert Mead, who transcended the individualist strains of American ideology and philosophy to emphasize the ways that self-identity is constructed through engagement with community. She came to Detroit in the aftermath of World War II, a period of time when the prospects for social democracy seemed greatest because of the complementary functioning of three pillars of society. Through wise investments, industrial capitalists would put the resources of nature and the labor of man to increasingly productive uses. Through thoughtful intervention, the state would regulate industry and redistribute wealth to promote the general good. And through dedicated organizing, the workers and the masses would build institutions to ensure their collective power was felt at the bargaining table, in the halls of government, and even in the direct ordering of the production process.

There was at best, however, a tentative agreement among these elements. In truth, none of them fully embraced the idea of social democracy: not the capitalists, who preferred to go about their dealings unfettered by a social contract; not the politicians, who grew wary of both Eastern and Western notions of "socialism" once the immediate crises of the Depression and World War II passed; and not even the U.S. workers, whose traditions of solidarity have always been complicated by race, gender, empire, and individualist notions of upward mobility.

The only certainty with capitalism is that it never stands still. It mandates that all who partake in the system engage in a process of constant and unending accumulation lest they be bulldozed in the path of creative destruction. Hence, the security, stability, and prosperity of postwar Detroit would prove fleeting or illusory. Indeed, Grace's 1953 arrival would mark the dawn of the city's most tumultuous period—and not coincidentally in the eyes of some observers.

In the quest for heightened productivity, the industries began replacing assembly-line workers with automated machines. At the same time, their desire for more cost-efficient plants, tax abatements, and greater leverage over the workforce led them to relocate production to the suburbs and to the Sunbelt, beginning a process that would eventually lead to international outsourcing. Not content with the proceeds of domestic sales, the Big 3 and other multinational corporations also supported an interventionist foreign policy whose "free market" objective was less the expansion of true democracy and more the capture of natural resources and expansion of outlets for U.S. goods.

The new contradictions soon sharpened within the trade union movement. In the aftermath of the 1950 labor-management accord, dubbed the Treaty of Detroit, too many trade union leaders began to fashion themselves as a labor aristocracy, turning their backs on the movement-building solidarity that had been their key source of power and remaking "big labor" into an interest group guided by its own "business" pursuits. After joining forces to kick the Reds out of the unions, these sorts of union officials united with management to support the American pursuit of global hegemony, which both agreed was the key to ever-rising profits and wages.

The giant triplets had taken firm hold. Marked by the achievement of a middle-class standard of living for millions of workers, the American Dream had grown increasingly corrupted by crass materialism. The high-minded notion of the "arsenal of democracy" to defeat Hitler and Tojo was now clouded by the recognition that militarism was a profitable enterprise. And in a Detroit where the black population was rapidly expanding while racial segregation remained the norm and public authorities remained overwhelmingly white, racial conflict was ready to explode.

Jimmy Boggs was a firsthand witness to the entrenched racism that pervaded the plant. Although discrimination had been far from eradicated by labor's winning of collective bargaining rights, the rise of the United Auto Workers (UAW) had carried with it rising expectations for African American workers and their families. By the 1960s, however, as automation was putting a halt to the expansion of opportunities, growing ranks within the black community became impatient with progress long stalled and bureaucratic structures that inhibited their democratic participation in the union. Hence, Jimmy and Grace Lee Boggs, joined by young militants in organizations such as the Dodge Revolutionary Union Movement (DRUM), encouraged protests against the old union leaders and called on blacks to seize the revolutionary role that only those standing outside of a corrupt and decaying system could play.

Racism was arguably more pervasive outside the plant. White flight from Detroit had been under way by the 1950s, producing racial and class segregation on a wider metropolitan scale. These white residents did not just follow the factory jobs to the suburbs. They were in large measure subsidized by the government to do so. Federal funding of the interstate highways, whose routes often deliberately tore through communities of color, literally paved the way for white flight. At the same time, federally guaranteed mortgages issued by the Federal Housing Authority and Veterans Administration made home ownership accessible to millions of Americans living in neighborhoods that were restricted to whites through overt measures such as restrictive covenants (contracts signed by property owners in all-white neighborhoods prohibiting the sale of homes to nonwhites) and through the stealthy acts of realtors and neighbors.

With Detroit on the cusp of becoming a majority black city by the mid-1960s, James and Grace Lee Boggs stood at the forefront of those issuing calls for Black Power. So when black frustration with racism, police abuse, and structural poverty erupted in the rebellion of 1967, the esteemed African American journalist Louis Lomax wrote in a feature for the *Detroit News* that "John *[sic]* Boggs and his Chinese wife, Grace Lee Boggs" were two of the six persons whom "Detroit's responsible Negroes [were] casting a jaundiced eye at" for having incited the rebellion.[5] With the rebellion hastening both white flight and black political ascendancy, Detroit elected its first black mayor. Coleman A. Young began his five terms as mayor in 1974, just as the city and the auto industry were entering a three-decade crisis of proportions few could envision.

Albeit urgent and overdue, black political power proved to be no antidote to the giant triplets. Racial tensions underlay the low-intensity war between Detroit and its predominantly white suburbs, which became the new base of support for Reagan's militaristic rhetoric. And even as the wealth evaporated in Detroit, materialist aspirations drove a new wave of violence and alienation in city and suburb alike.

Confronting new challenges, the Boggses' thinking adapted to a changing reality. They declared that the welfare state, the New Left, and the Black Power movement had all run their course. Thus, it was now necessary to move from redistributive justice to rebuilding our cities and reconstructing human relations from the ground up. This would mandate going beyond the politics of minority grievance to developing multiracial strategies to combat a system that was multinational in scope. And despite the rising domestic despair and global anger at Yankee imperialism, it was incumbent on U.S. revolutionaries to "love America enough to change it." This meant creating models of work, education, art, and community that would transform those rebels filled with righteous anger into productive change agents who understood that self-transformation and structural transformation must go hand in hand. As Gandhi said and King concurred, you must be the change you wish to see in the world. In words that will resonate throughout this book, we must define revolution both by the humanity-stretching *ends* to be achieved and the beloved community-building *means* by which to achieve those ends.

The Motor City, even dating back to the heyday of the domestic auto industry, has long been scarred by perpetual divisions of race, class, and geography. Today, with the Big 3 automakers a shadow of their former selves, the entire region lives under a dark cloud of insecurity while large swaths of inner-city Detroit—areas marked by an exodus of stable homes and businesses—have fallen completely off the radar screen of mainstream society. Schools are failing miserably and human services have been stripped to a bare minimum. The ranks of the school dropouts, functionally illiterate, and structurally unemployed increase every year.

Before connecting with Grace, I had given Detroit scant consideration, either as a contemporary or as a historical entity. What strikes just about every visitor from outside the city upon arrival is the physical evidence of abandonment and devastation. The vacant lots, burned-out buildings, and boarded historical edifices are everywhere. One immediately thinks of all the things that are missing, especially basic signs of retail commerce— malls, department stores, supermarkets, big-box stores, and other standard trappings of the American landscape. Even mom-and-pop shops (save liquor stores) are difficult to find in many neighborhoods. The images of poverty, inequality, and segregation one gets from even the most rudimentary tour of Detroit are vital. They offer penetrating insights into the decay of industrial society, a place where big capitalism has lost all sense of creativity but retains all of its destructive capacities. Detroit provides a firsthand look at a dying order.

But such a vantage point falls quick prey to voyeurism and exploitation. What we must also see in Detroit is the prospect of living radically differently, when necessity and possibility combine to facilitate the beginning of a rupture with the culture of the industrial age. Since traditional forms of politics (including ostensibly oppositional forms) have failed so fantastically in Detroit, a qualitatively different kind of activism has taken root in the city, epitomized by organizations such as the youth leadership movement, Detroit Summer. Their work may appear small scale and the change they bring incremental: here a mural; there a community garden; a collection of poems or songs documenting the ideas of youth. But what they foster is an enduring spirit of humanism whose essence this book seeks to capture. Out of the depths of poverty, segregation, despair, abandonment, pollution, and marginalization, grassroots activists are bringing to life projects and movements that while local in scope are projecting and shining a light on the fundamental human values of hope, cooperation, stewardship, and respect. It is in this regard that we have come to see the sprouting of a farm in the middle of a concrete jungle as transformative in ways that even a large mass protest is not. As Grace argues, echoing author Margaret Wheatley, movements are born of critical connections rather than critical mass.

The instilling of these humanist values through such small-scale but easily replicated projects leads us to believe that the twenty-first century holds dramatically brighter prospects than the current crises might suggest. As such, a new wave of visitors—many stopping at the corner of Field and Goethe to soak up Grace's thoughts—has descended on Detroit to discover critical connections. "Detroit is where change is most urgent and therefore most viable," author Rebecca Solnit wrote in 2007 after completing a tour of many of the sites discussed in this book. "The rest of us will get there later, when necessity drives us too, and by that time Detroit may be the shining example we can look to, the post-industrial green city that was once the steel-grey capital of Fordist manufacturing."[6]

Even skeptics are taking notice. A spring 2009 article by the establishment-minded *Time* magazine characterized Detroit as "a laboratory for the sort of radical reconstruction needed to fend off urban decline." Later that year, Time Inc. stationed a team of reporters from its family of publications to live in a house on Detroit's Eastside and cover the city up close for an entire year. Top editor John Huey explained, "From urban planning to the crisis of manufacturing, from the lingering role of race and class in our society to the struggle for better health care and education, it's all happening at its most extreme in the Motor City."[7]

After a March 2009 visit to an urban farm in Detroit, John Reed wrote in London's venerable business publication the *Financial Times:* "In an earlier time, I might have lost patience with these eco-centric, anti-globalisation arguments. This winter, in Detroit, they sounded right. At a time when jobs and whole industries are collapsing, growing your own food seems reasonable."[8]

The American Dream is dead. Long live the American Dream.

AMERICA BEYOND 2008

What time is it on the clock of the world?

Grace regularly opens meetings and conversations by posing this question. In part, she implores us to think globally about social conditions and to see our interconnection with all beings of the Earth. Above all, she challenges us to think philosophically about our place in human history and the role we must play in shaping the future. We are living through a quintessential moment of crisis representing both danger and opportunity. The economic meltdown and ongoing wars are wrecking havoc on the lives of millions, especially those already bearing the greatest brunt of oppression. But Grace insists that we do more than denounce the crimes of those in power and demand quick fixes. I want to offer a taste of what Grace calls "the sense of history" we need to have as we assess the present moment.

There is a reason why Americans are so deeply committed to divesting themselves from the problems facing Detroit. As Jerry Herron notes, Detroit is "the place where bad times get sent to make them belong to somebody else."[9] Detroit's downfall from its own "golden age" reminds us that we are no longer in the golden age of American capitalism: when U.S. hegemony and comparative advantage allowed the Big 3 auto companies to dominate the global market share; when U.S. foreign policy makers could rest assured that most of the world either feared or respected American power; when U.S. industry could still incorporate new sectors of the working class into its fold and devote a portion of its inflated profits to buying social peace; and when the negative environmental consequences of industrialism could be set aside for future generations to worry about. Jimmy and Grace foresaw these developments four decades ago, but what her interlocutor Immanuel Wallerstein has characterized as "the decline of American power" is now increasingly evident to all but the most hardened neoconservative observers.[10] Moreover, the withdrawal from the nation's key social investments (most notably, public education) does not augur well for a resurgence.

As Grace recounts in the pages that follow, Detroit's history is embedded with struggles that expose the contradictions inherent in the golden age. However, the city's deep despair further reminds us that, over the past four decades, the U.S. public has largely evaded responsibility for confronting the giant triplets of racism, militarism, and materialism. Because of that evasion, history took another course. As Thatcherism and Reaganism crystallized the backlash to the new social movements and national liberation struggles of the 1960s and 1970s, conservative forces advanced a neoliberal agenda worldwide. "There is no alternative" to the dictates of global capital and finance went their rallying cry, as they lorded over privatization and deregulation while imposing "austerity" on the working class and unmaking the welfare state.

In defiance of such hubris, Grace's vision of the next American Revolution is driven by the belief that "Another World Is Possible"—the marching banner of the new global movement that has arisen over the past decade and a slogan that quickly became one of Grace's most repeated phrases to young activists. The demise of the neoliberal consensus was hastened by the undoing of two outlandishly excessive schemes: the Bush administration's neoconservatives championing U.S. exceptionalism and reckless militarism while vowing to remake the Middle East in America's image; and Wall Street's "masters of the universe" sucking most of the global economy into a multitrillion-dollar Ponzi scheme. We can see the upshot clearly in Latin America, where left-leaning governments have now taken power throughout much of the region, awakening new hopes for social change while prompting new challenges for leaders and movements.

Emphasizing the dynamic role of human–change agents, Grace draws special attention to the impact that the 1999 "Battle of Seattle" demonstrations against the World Trade Organization and corporate globalization made in breaking through the neoliberal consensus. This historic act of rebellion was followed by the proactive and forward-looking World Social Forums, which first gathered in Porto Alegre, Brazil, in 2001. Nine years later the regional branch of this movement came to Detroit, where Grace sat center stage as eighteen thousand activists coalesced for the second United States Social Forum.

Convening amid the ruins of industry and in the shadow of financial calamity, the Detroit forum amplified Grace's fundamental message that we must view the present period as one of liberation—from the teleological view of progress, from the dehumanization of the industrial age, and from the burdens of empire. This is a period that provides every one of us with the opportunity to participate in a drama of world-historic political and cultural implications. We need to be very clear, she asserts, that the "hard times" we are in represent a protracted period of "growing pains" and cannot be measured in months or years.

The core mission of this book is to help us comprehend the epochal shift that confronts us at the dawn of the new millennium and to help project and guide the actions we must urgently take. We need to have a clear sense of what is dying, what is growing, and what has yet to be born in this phase of transition. We must move toward the future lacking a clear-cut blueprint of what is to be done and shedding a dogmatic sense of the eternal truth but carrying with us a shared sense of the awareness, values, methods, and relationships necessary to navigate these uncharted waters.

To set off on the right track, we need to embrace Grace's imperative to think dialectically about the confluence of forces that have brought us to this turning point. On the surface, it seems obvious that the social crises and human catastrophes haunting us today can be linked to the presidency of George W. Bush—his blind pursuit of war, blissful ignorance of our planetary crisis, warped economic policies, callous disregard for the Constitution, and clueless response to Hurricane Katrina. Still, placed into proper perspective, Bush represents far more than an eight-year mistake. As Grace argues, Bush represents the end of an era—one dating back to the advent of capitalism and taking off with the rise of industrial society. Through this modern era, to which belongs the entire history of the United States as a sovereign entity, a growing proportion of human civilization came to define progress by the acquisition of wealth and by ever-expanding growth in production and consumption. Now, as hundreds of millions of Chinese, Indians, and other peoples in what was once called the Third World rush to garner the virtues of capitalist accumulation, the limits of an industrial order are clearly on the horizon.

As Grace inspires us to be the change we wish to see in the world, she demands that we appreciate how we are all in some way implicated in the production of this mess we find ourselves in. As the old idea of the welfare state and its guarantee of a social safety net receded, we have become increasingly subject to market forces and corporate influence. Local and state governments, public school districts and universities, workers' pension funds, and municipal transit agencies across the United States have endured massive budget cuts and huge deficits because their finances had become directly and indirectly bound to the casino economy and its culture of easy money. Our home mortgages are now routinely converted into bonds, whose values then become the source of high-stakes gambling in the form of derivative trading. Thus, even if we have never invested a single dollar of our own funds in the stock market, we find our fates entangled with those of Wall Street investment banks, hedge funds, and insurance conglomerates like AIG.

Drawing on her humanist readings of Karl Marx, Grace urges us to analyze not only the material forms of inequality caused by capitalism but also the dehumanization and spiritual impoverishment inherent in a society dominated by money relations. As the professional class pursued higher bonuses and paychecks and the working class became reliant on more family members working longer hours, the combined result was the commodification of ever-greater spheres of life. Our communal care system built on extended family networks has substantially given way to paid child care and paid elder care. Even when we are wholesome enough to eat our vegetables, we increasingly buy prepackaged, prewashed, and precut produce that relies on the paid labor of workers whom we never see. Those of us who seek nothing but nurturing toys for our children are now realizing that these too are likely to be tied up in a chaotic global industrialization process—one that has not only produced lead-painted Doras and Elmos but also corrupted domestic and international food supplies. Binding all of these phenomena together is the production and exploitation of "cheap" labor—women, people of color, immigrants, rural-to-urban migrants—those literally and figuratively displaced from their communities by corporate globalization. Being a more conscious consumer (e.g., buying local and organic) is imperative but not nearly sufficient. To confront our problems, we must break with the cult of economic growth, resist xenophobic scapegoating, and realize there is no technological fix that will restore our profligate ways of the late twentieth century.

Once we appreciate the true symbolism of Bush as the end of one era, we can better appreciate the new possibilities and tensions marking the dawn of the Obama era. Obama's inspiring, hope-filled campaign was a clear sign of how demographic and cultural changes are reshaping U.S. politics. His captivating personal background, deep and thoughtful writings, and poetic and uplifting speeches excited and electrified Americans who had felt ignored, exploited, and belittled by politicians their entire lives. Obama especially helped communities of color and young people believe that real and meaningful political change was within their grasp.

But what really made 2008 a breakthrough year was the way in which those millions and millions of believers put their hopes into action—not just by voting in record numbers but also by reading and studying, writing and blogging, calling and texting, and ultimately going door-to-door to every stretch of every state in the Union to spread a message of change we can believe in. Our system of representative democracy, itself a product of the first American Revolution of 1776, trains us to focus on the results of elections. Most Americans equate democracy with voting, and they expect their elected officials to do their bidding once they put them into office. But as Grace asserts, that system, while it still has room for some admirable individuals, has been thoroughly corrupted by what the Zapatistas call the "Empire of Money."

While some look to Obama to rescue *representative* democracy, we need to focus on how the grassroots movement underlying his campaign advanced new expressions of *participatory* democracy that are pivotal to the next American Revolution. Over the long haul, the campaign of 2008 will prove meaningful only if it is part and parcel of a broader movement to launch what Grace calls "a new more earth-centered, more community-centered and more democratic epoch." Building this movement transcends who is president and whether Republicans or Democrats are in the majority. We need to appreciate our capacity to make choices and take actions that can bring about true change from the ground up. This means that we must understand and struggle through the new contradictions that have come to the fore with the United States' first black president.

We need to see beyond those progressive-minded persons who, having devoted their lives to the cause of antiracism, are fixated on the obvious—that racism persists and that too many Americans want to point to Obama's election to claim racism has been vanquished. Aiding this effort are those vocal reactionary elements—Grace calls them "counterrevolutionary" forces—such as Sarah Palin, Glenn Beck, and the "birthers" who rail against all those ("socialists," "foreigners," "illegal aliens") they see destroying their notion of the "real America." While a minority, these forces, particularly their most violent and alienated strains, do constitute a real danger and must be dealt with. But as Grace argues, those of us who care about transforming society must use the "whip of the counterrevolution" productively. We cannot wed ourselves to an endless protest against the most backward elements of society.

It is easy to unite against that which you are *against*. Hence, the Bush era produced heightened cooperation between liberals, progressives, and radicals. Grace directs our focus to the greater task: defining what we are *for* while enacting proposals to govern the whole of society. We cannot do this unless we are willing and able to develop nonantagonistic means to struggle among ourselves, to struggle against our own outmoded concepts and practices while working to unleash new creative energies.

We must seize the opportunity to redefine the meaning of "majority rule," which has been bound to the concept of America as a white majority society, as well as a generally patriarchal society, since the origins of the nation. Thus, all who have defined ourselves as the "oppressed" will be increasingly empowered to break free of what Jimmy Boggs called the underling mentality of a minority and to become what Grace calls "active citizens, builders of a new America that all of us will be proud to call our own." This means enhancing our capacities for self-government rather than simply demanding and expecting that our elected representatives take care of us. She is thus less than content with the liberal/progressive demands for the federal government to provide a bigger stimulus, boost consumer spending, expand health insurance, and increase the competitiveness of U.S. industry. In her eyes they are, at best, Band-Aid reforms and, at worst, distortions of the task at hand. While clearly superior to Bush's agenda, they reflect an anachronistic yearning for social democracy.

At the same time, Grace reminds us that we cannot allow innocent notions of hope and empowerment to go unquestioned. We need to challenge those who see the dawn of the Obama era as an opportunity to move up within the system. Every time a new barrier is broken, there will be many new openings for people of color, women, the disabled, and queer folk to situate themselves on the wrong side of history. We also need to challenge those whose enthrallment with what Obama represents culturally—that is, the vitality of youth, the rhetoric of a community organizer, the sanctity of the black family, the rhythm of hip-hop—inhibits their ability to think critically about politics.

So it is perfectly clear, let me close by reiterating the assertion that will resonate throughout this book: the change needed to overcome our mounting crises must be of revolutionary scale. This book provides a particular vision of radical change and explains how it grew out of historic movements against racism, materialism, and militarism. It further demonstrates how that vision is being enacted today through struggles to revitalize inner-city neighborhoods, build community, reconnect with the Earth, and transform our schools. In this sense, it is written with an activist audience in mind. We hope it will make its way into the hands of people with the courage and conviction to dedicate their lives to making the world anew and better.

But it is not only or even primarily designed for self-defined or self-styled activists, for we believe everyone in their daily practice—as parents and children, as politicians and voters, as teachers and preachers, as artists and scientists, as neighbors and friends, and so on—has both the ability and the responsibility to change the way we relate individually and collectively to each other and to our social world. Moreover, unlike some works whose purpose is primarily to embolden activists to fight longer and harder, we make a point of criticizing a number of problematic tendencies we have witnessed among left-wing activists, especially the impulse to react and protest without properly thinking through situations and taking the time to project viable alternatives. Revolution, as Grace emphasizes, is not a onetime, D-day event that will happen when a critical mass of forces takes the correct action at the proper time. It is a protracted process tied to slower evolutionary changes that cannot be dismissed.

More than anything else, tackling a systemic crisis and moving from degeneration to reconstruction requires us to be creative in a dual sense. These perilous times call for us to be both imaginative and generative. Time is precious. History awaits our response.

CHAPTER ONE

These Are the Times
to Grow Our Souls

On June 27, 2010, I celebrated my ninety-fifth birthday. Over the past few years I have become much less mobile. I no longer bound from my chair to fetch a book or article to show a visitor. I have two hearing aids, three pairs of glasses, and very few teeth. But I still have most of my marbles, mainly because I am good at learning, arguably the most important qualification for a movement activist. In fact, the past decade-plus since the 1998 publication of my autobiography, *Living for Change,* has been one of the busiest and most invigorating periods of my life.

I have a lot to learn from. I was born during World War I, above my father's Chinese American restaurant in downtown Providence, Rhode Island. This means that through no fault of my own, I have lived through most of the catastrophic events of the twentieth century—the Great Depression, fascism and Nazism, the Holocaust, World War II, the A-bomb and the H-bomb, Hiroshima and Nagasaki, the cold war, the Korean War, McCarthyism, the Vietnam War, 9/11, and the "taking the law into our own hands" response of the Bush administration. Perhaps eighty million people have been killed in wars during my lifetime.

But it has also been my good fortune to have lived long enough to witness the death blow dealt to the illusion that unceasing technological innovations and economic growth can guarantee happiness and security to the citizens of our planet's only superpower.

Since I left the university in 1940, I have been privileged to participate in most of the great humanizing movements of the past seventy years—the labor, civil rights, Black Power, women's, Asian American, environmental justice, and antiwar movements. Each of these has been a tremendously transformative experience for me, expanding my understanding of what it means to be both an American and a human being, while challenging me to keep deepening my thinking about how to bring about radical social change.

However, I cannot recall any previous period when the issues were so basic, so interconnected, and so demanding of everyone living in this country, regardless of race, ethnicity, class, gender, age, or national origin. At this point in the continuing evolution of our country and of the human race, we urgently need to stop thinking of ourselves as victims and to recognize that we must each become a part of the solution because we are each a part of the problem.

What is our response to the economic crisis and financial meltdown? Will we just keep scrambling to react to each new domino that falls (e.g., Bear Stearns, Lehman Brothers, Fannie/Freddie, AIG, Citigroup)? Or are we prepared to develop a whole new form of solidarity economics emphasizing sustainability, mutuality, and local self-reliance?

How are we going to make our living in an age when Hi-Tech (high technology) and the export of jobs overseas have brought us to the point where the number of workers needed to produce goods and services is constantly diminishing? Where will we get the imagination, the courage, and the determination to reconceptualize the meaning and purpose of Work in a society that is becoming increasingly jobless?

What is going to happen to cities like Detroit, which was once the "arsenal of democracy," and others whose apex was tied to manufacturing? Now that they've been abandoned by industry, are we just going to throw them away? Or can we rebuild, redefine, and respirit them as models of twenty-first-century self-reliant and sustainable multicultural communities? Who is going to begin this new story?

How are we going to redefine Education so that half of all inner-city children do not drop out of school, thus ensuring that large numbers will end up in prison? Is it enough to call for "Education, not Incarceration"? Or does our top-down educational system, created a hundred years ago to prepare an immigrant population for factory work, bear a large part of the responsibility for the atrocity that, even though the United States is home to less than 5 percent of the world's total population, we are responsible for nearly 25 percent of the world's incarcerated population?

How are we going to build a twenty-first-century America in which people of all races and ethnicities live together in harmony, and European Americans in particular embrace their new role as one among many minorities constituting the new multiethnic majority?

What is going to motivate us to start caring for our biosphere instead of using our mastery of technology to increase the volume and speed at which we are making our planet uninhabitable for other species and eventually for ourselves?

And, especially since 9/11, how are we to achieve reconciliation with the two-thirds of the world that increasingly resents our economic, military, and cultural domination? Can we accept their anger as a challenge rather than a threat? Out of our new vulnerability can we recognize that our safety now depends on our loving and caring for the peoples of the world as we love and care for our own families? Or can we conceive of security only in terms of the Patriot Act and the exercising of our formidable military power?

Where will we get the courage and the imagination to free ourselves from the quagmires of Iraq and Afghanistan, the wars that have killed tens of thousands while squandering hundreds of billions of dollars? What will help us confront our own hubris, our own irresponsibility, and our own unwillingness, as individuals and as a nation, to engage in seeking radical solutions to the growing inequality between the nations of the North and those of the South? Can we create a new paradigm of our selfhood and our nationhood? Or are we so locked into nationalism, racism, and determinism that we will be driven to seek scapegoats for our frustrations and failures as the Germans did after World War I, thus aiding and abetting the onset of Hitler and the Holocaust?[1]

We live at a very dangerous time because these questions are no longer abstractions. As we embrace the challenges and opportunities awaiting us in the age of Obama, we must be mindful of the mess we are in and the damage we must undo. Our political system became so undemocratic and dysfunctional that we were saddled with a president unable to distinguish between facts and personal fantasies. Eight years of George W. Bush left us stuck in two wars. Under the guise of defense against terrorism, our government violated the Geneva Conventions and the U.S. Constitution, torturing detainees, suspending habeas corpus, and instituting warrantless domestic spying. Meanwhile, our media are owned and controlled by huge multinational corporations who treat the American people as consumers and audience rather than as active citizens.

Our heedless pursuit of material and technological growth has created a planetary emergency. With places such as the Maldives—the islands that scientists warn may be engulfed by rising seas—confronting a threat to their existence and the livelihoods of millions more being undermined, "climate justice" promises to be the defining issue of the twenty-first century. The physical threat posed by climate change represents a crisis that is not only material but also profoundly spiritual at its core because it challenges us to think seriously about the future of the human race and what it means to be a human being. Our lives, the lives of our children and of future generations, and even the survival of life on Earth depend on our willingness to transform ourselves into active planetary and global citizens who, as Martin Luther King Jr. put it, "develop an overriding loyalty to mankind as a whole in order to preserve the best in their individual societies."[2]

The time is already very late and we have a long way to go to meet these challenges. In the decades following World War II, the so-called American Century gave rise to an economic expansion that has ultimately driven us further apart rather than closer together. Growing inequality in the United States, which is now the most stratified among industrialized nations, has made a mockery of our founding ideals. CEOs of failed financial institutions have walked away with ill-gotten fortunes. Millions of children in the Global South die each year of starvation while diabetes as a result of obesity is approaching epidemic levels in the United States.

Yet rather than wrestle with such grim realities, too many Americans have become self-centered and overly materialistic, more concerned with our possessions and individual careers than with the state of our neighborhoods, cities, country, and planet, closing our eyes and hearts to the many forms of violence that have been exploding in our inner cities and in powder kegs all over the rest of the world. Because the problems seem so insurmountable and because just struggling for our own survival consumes so much of our time and energy, we view ourselves as victims rather than embrace the power within us to change our reality.

Over the past seventy years the various identity struggles have to some degree remediated the great wrongs that have been done to workers, people of color, Indigenous Peoples, women, gays and lesbians, and the disabled, while helping to humanize our society overall. But they have also had a shadow side in the sense that they have encouraged us to think of ourselves more as determined than as self-determining, more as victims of "isms" (racism, sexism, capitalism, ableism) than as human beings who have the power of choice. For our own survival we must assume individual and collective responsibility for creating a new nation—one that is loved rather than feared and one that does not have to bribe and bully other nations to win support.

These are the times that try our souls. Each of us needs to undergo a tremendous philosophical and spiritual transformation. Each of us needs to be awakened to a personal and compassionate recognition of the inseparable interconnection between our minds, hearts, and bodies; between our physical and psychical well-being; and between our selves and all the other selves in our country and in the world. Each of us needs to stop being a passive observer of the suffering that we know is going on in the world and start identifying with the sufferers. Each of us needs to make a leap that is both practical and philosophical, beyond determinism to self-determination. Each of us has to be true to and enhance our own humanity by embracing and practicing the conviction that as human beings we have Free Will.

Despite the powers and principles that are bent on objectifying and commodifying us and all our human relationships, the interlocking crises of our time require that we exercise the power within us to make principled choices in our ongoing daily and political lives—choices that will eventually although not inevitably (since there are no guarantees) make a difference.

AN END TO POLITICS AS USUAL

How are we going to bring about these transformations? Politics as usual—debate and argument, even voting—are no longer sufficient. Our system of representative democracy, created by a great revolution, must now itself become the target of revolutionary change. For too many years counting, vast numbers of people stopped going to the polls, either because they did not care what happened to the country or the world or because they did not believe that voting would make a difference on the profound and interconnected issues that really matter. Now, with a surge of new political interest having give rise to the Obama presidency, we need to inject new meaning into the concept of the "will of the people."

The will of too many Americans has been to pursue private happiness and take as little responsibility as possible for governing our country. As a result, we have left the job of governing to our elected representatives, even though we know that they serve corporate interests and therefore make decisions that threaten our biosphere and widen the gulf between the rich and poor both in our country and throughout the world. In other words, even though it is readily apparent that our lifestyle choices and the decisions of our representatives are increasing social injustice and endangering our planet, too many of us have wanted to continue going our merry and not-so-merry ways, periodically voting politicians in and out of office but leaving the responsibility for policy decisions to them. Our will has been to act like consumers, not like responsible citizens.

Historians may one day look back at the 2000 election, marked by the Supreme Court's decision to award the presidency to George W. Bush, as a decisive turning point in the death of representative democracy in the United States. National Public Radio analyst Daniel Schorr called it "a junta." Jack Lessenberry, columnist for the *MetroTimes* in Detroit, called it "a right-wing judicial coup." Although more restrained, the language of dissenting justices Breyer, Ginsberg, Souter, and Stevens was equally clear. They said that there was no legal or moral justification for deciding the presidency in this way.[3]

That's why Al Gore didn't speak for me in his concession speech. You don't just "strongly disagree" with a right-wing coup or a junta. You expose it as illegal, immoral, and illegitimate, and you start building a movement to challenge and change the system that created it. The crisis brought on by the fraud of 2000 and aggravated by the Bush administration's constant and callous disregard for the Constitution exposed so many defects that we now have an unprecedented opportunity not only to improve voting procedures but to turn U.S. democracy into "government of the people, by the people, and for the people" instead of government of, by, and for corporate power.

We may take some brief solace in the fact that George W. Bush's terms in office, while wreaking national and global havoc, aroused heightened political awareness and opposition. Tens of thousands in Washington, DC, and other cities across the country denounced him through a counterinaugural. Then beginning in 2002, millions more took to the streets at home and abroad to denounce the war in Iraq. Meanwhile, the needless death and suffering that occurred in the aftermath of Hurricane Katrina exposed the true depths of corruption, incompetence, and arrogance within the administration.

Still, it becomes clearer every day that organizing or joining massive protests and demanding new policies fail to sufficiently address the crisis we face. They may demonstrate that we are on the right side politically, but they are not transformative enough. They do not change the cultural images or the symbols that play such a pivotal role in molding us into who we are.

GROWING OUR SOULS

Art can help us to envision the new cultural images we need to grow our souls. As the labor movement was developing in the pre–World War II years, John Steinbeck's *Grapes of Wrath* transformed the way that Americans viewed themselves in relationship to faceless bankers and heartless landowners. In the 1970s and 1980s artist Judy Chicago's exhibits, *The Dinner Party* and *Birth Project,* reimagined the vagina, transforming it from a private space and site of oppression into a public space of beauty and spiritual as well as physical creation and liberation. In this period, we need artists to create new images that will liberate us from our preoccupation with constantly expanding production and consumption and open up space in our hearts and minds to imagine and create another America that will be viewed by the world as a beacon rather than as a danger.

This need has become more urgent since September 11, 2001. The activist, organizer, and writer Starhawk writes that "911 threw us collectively into a deep well of grief." "The movement we need to build now," she argues, "the potential for transformation that might arise out of this tragedy, must speak to the heart of the pain we share across political lines. A great hole has been torn out of the heart of the world." This potential can be realized only when we summon the courage to confront "a fear more profound than even the terror caused by the attack itself. For those towers represented human triumph over nature. Larger than life, built to be unburnable, they were the *Titanic* of our day."

"Faced with the profundity of loss, with the stark reality of death, we find words inadequate," Starhawk further notes. "The language of abstraction doesn't work. Ideology doesn't work. Judgment and hectoring and shaming and blaming cannot truly touch the depth of that loss. Only poetry can address grief. Only words that convey what we can see and smell and taste and touch of life, can move us." "To do that," she concludes, "we need to forge a new language of both the word and the deed."[4]

The America that is best known and most resented around the world pursues unlimited economic growth, technological revolutions, and consumption, with little or no regard for their destructive impact on communities, on the environment, and on the billions of people who live in what used to be called the "Third World."

However, the end of the Bush regime provides an opening to build national and international recognition of the movement to "grow our souls," which began emerging organically in the United States in the aftermath of World War II. The dropping of the atom bomb on Hiroshima and Nagasaki demonstrated the enormous power and the enormous limitations of viewing human beings primarily as producers and as rational beings in the scientific sense. At the time, Einstein remarked, "The unleashed power of the atom bomb has changed everything except our modes of thinking, and thus we drift toward unparalleled catastrophes." Thus, he recognized the urgent need for us to redefine what it means to be a human being. Warning about the danger of unfettered technological progress, Einstein asserted that the solution of world peace could arise only from inside the hearts of humankind. That is why "imagination is more important than knowledge."[5]

"A human being," Einstein concluded, "is a part of the whole, called by us 'Universe,' a part limited in time and space. He experiences himself, his thoughts and feelings as something separated from the rest—a kind of optical delusion of his consciousness. This delusion is a kind of prison for us, restricting us to our personal desires and to affection for a few persons nearest to us. Our task must be to free ourselves from this prison by widening our circle of compassion to embrace all living creatures and the whole of nature in its beauty."[6]

The nuclear bomb created a Great Divide in theories and strategies for social change. Henceforth, human beings could no longer pretend that everything that happened to us was determined by external or economic circumstances. Freedom now included the responsibility for making choices. Radical social change could no longer be viewed in terms of transferring power from the top to the bottom or of simple binary oppositions— us versus them, victims versus villains, good versus evil. We could no longer afford a separation between politics and ethics. Within the Marxist-Leninist paradigm, consciousness and self-consciousness and ideas and values were mere "superstructure." Now they had to become integral, both as end and as means, to social struggle. Radical social change had to be viewed as a two-sided transformational process, of ourselves and of our institutions, a process requiring protracted struggle and not just a D-day replacement of one set of rulers with another.

The Montgomery Bus Boycott of 1955–56 was the first struggle by an oppressed people in Western society from this new philosophical/political perspective. Before the eyes of the whole world, a people who had been treated as less than human struggled against their dehumanization not as angry victims or rebels but as new men and women, representative of a new, more human society. Practicing methods of nonviolence that transformed themselves and increased the good rather than the evil in the world and always bearing in mind that their goal was not only desegregating the buses but creating the beloved community, they inspired the human identity and ecological movements that over the past forty years have been creating a new civil society in the United States.

The sermons of Martin Luther King Jr. and other religious leaders, produced in the heat of struggle, played a critical role in the success of the Montgomery boycott and ensuing civil rights struggles. But as my friend the late Rosemarie Freeney Harding, who worked closely with Student Nonviolent Coordinating Committee activists in the 1960s, pointed out, "Another vital source of support was music, particularly the sacred music of the black experience, which has long been an alchemical resource for struggle: a conjured strength." Harding concluded, "The songs changed the atmosphere, becoming an almost palpable barrier between demonstrators and police, giving the marchers an internal girding that allowed them to move without fear."[7]

I recall how activists popularized songs like "Joe Hill" and "Solidarity Forever" in the decades before the civil rights movement, thus demonstrating the link between music and social action. But the songs of the civil rights movement, such as "We Shall Overcome" and "Ain't Gonna Let Nobody Turn Me Around," did more than energize those on the front lines. They helped grow the souls of their supporters all over the world.

The publication of Rachel Carson's *Silent Spring* in 1962 added another dimension to the evolving movement toward inner and outer transformation initiated by the civil rights movement. By helping us to see how the widespread use of chemicals and hazardous technologies in post–World War II America was silencing "robins, catbirds, doves, jays, wrens and scores of other bird voices," Carson awakened millions of Americans to the sacredness of Nature and to the need, expressed by Einstein, for "widening our circle of compassion to embrace all living creatures and the whole of nature in its beauty."[8]

The next year Betty Friedan's *The Feminine Mystique* brought small groups of women together in consciousness-raising groups all over the country. Laughing and crying over stories of growing up female in a patriarchal society, women turned anger into hope and created a social and political movement much more participatory and closer to daily life than just going to the polls and voting. The transformative power of women's storytelling has been captured by playwright Eve Ensler in *The Vagina Monologues,* a dramatic compilation of women's soliloquies. Every year, to raise both funds and consciousness, thousands of women's groups all over the country and the world reproduce—or produce their own version of—these monologues, turning the monologue art form itself into a movement.

As the civil rights movement, the environmental movement, and the women's movement were gaining momentum, small groups of individuals, especially on the West Coast, were coming together in workshops to open themselves up to new, more spiritual ways of knowing, consciously decentering the scientific rationalism that had laid the philosophic foundation for the modern age. To become truly human and to really know Truth, people discovered, we need to summon up all our mental and spiritual resources, constantly expanding our imaginations, sensitivities, and capacity for wonder and love, for hope rather than despair, for compassion and cooperation rather than cynicism and competition, for spiritual aspiration and moral effort. Instead of either/or, reductive, dualistic, and divisive, or "blaming the other," thinking, the movement affirmed the unity of mind and body and of the spiritual with the material. It advocated a consciousness that rejects determinism—the belief that we are limited by the past—and repudiates all absolutes. Instead, the movement promoted a consciousness that finds joy in crossing boundaries, is naturalistic instead of supernatural, and strives for empowerment rather than power and control.

TOWARD THE GREAT TURNING

All over the world, local groups are struggling, as we are in Detroit, to keep our communities, our environment, and our humanity from being destroyed by corporate globalization. In his book *Blessed Unrest*, environmentalist Paul Hawken estimates that there may be more than one million of these self-healing civic groups across every country around the world. Most of them are small and barely visible, but together they are creating the largest movement the world has ever known. Many of these groups are inspired by a philosophy that replaces the scientific and reductive rationalism of seventeenth-century Western male philosophers (such as Descartes and Bacon) with the ways of knowing of Indigenous Peoples (which include the perceptions of trees and animals) and of women, based on intimate connections with Nature and ideas of healing and caring that were part of European village culture prior to the sixteenth- and seventeenth-century witch hunts.[9]

This movement has no central leadership and is not bound together by any *ism.* Its very diverse and widely scattered individuals and groups are connected mainly by the Internet and other information technologies. But they are joined at the heart by their commitment to achieving social justice, establishing new forms of more democratic governance, and creating new ways of living at the local level that will reconnect us with the Earth and with one another. Above all, they are linked by their indomitable faith in our ability to create the world anew.

Millions of people in the United States are part of this organically evolving cultural revolution. Because we believe in combining spiritual growth and awakening with practical actions in our daily lives, we are having a profound effect on American culture. For example, most of us reject the getting and spending that not only lay waste to our own powers but also put intolerable pressures on the environment. We try to eat homegrown rather than processed foods and to maintain our physical well-being through healthful habits rather than by dependence on prescription drugs. Overall, we try to make our living in ways that are in harmony with our convictions.

Depending on skills, interests, and where we live, most of us carry on this cultural revolution in our own way. For example, a doctor may decide to practice alternative medicine. A teacher will try to create a more democratic classroom. A businessperson will try to replace competition with cooperation in his firm or may quit the business altogether to act as a consultant to community organizations. Whatever our line of work, we participate in a lot of workshops because we view our selves and the culture as works in progress.

The social activists among us struggle to create actions that go beyond protest and negativity and build community because community is the most important thing that has been destroyed by the dominant culture. For example, at mass demonstrations against the North American Free Trade Agreement (NAFTA) or corporate globalization, Starhawk organizes small affinity groups to promote democratic decision making and to combine community building with protest.

What unites us is not an organization or leaders but the sense that we are in the middle of what Buddhist writer Joanna Macy calls a "Great Turning."[10] We need to recognize that we are coming to the end of ten thousand years of agricultural and industrial society, both of which are patriarchal. Many of my European friends viewed George W. Bush as the last gasp of industrial society because he was so determined to pursue economic growth even at the risk of destroying our biosphere. We must see the need to confront the crises we face today as part of a broader challenge to make the transition to a new postindustrial world based on partnership among ourselves and with our environment rather than patriarchal and bureaucratic domination.

Whether or not the media recognize it, the Great Turning is a reality. Although we cannot know yet if it will take hold in time for humans and other complex life-forms to survive, we can know that it is under way. And it is gaining momentum, through the actions of countless individuals and groups around the world. To see this as the larger context of our lives clears our vision and summons our courage.

The writings of Karen Armstrong can help us put this notion of a Great Turning into further perspective. I discovered her work after 9/11, when I wanted to know more about Islam. Often called the "runaway nun," Armstrong left the convent in her early twenties, turning her back on the "narrow gate" of religion. Fifteen years later, while working on a film on Jerusalem, she started investigating the origins of Judaism. This led to her studying and writing readable books on the history of different religions.

In her book *The Great Transformation: The Beginning of Our Religious Traditions,* Armstrong explains how the great faiths (Hinduism, Buddhism, Confucianism, Judaism) emerged during the seven hundred years from 900 to 200 B.C. in countries like China and India. In this period, sometimes called the "Axial Age," societies on the Eurasian continent were undergoing a great transition: from tribalism, in which individuals were submerged in the community, to urban ways of living that challenged individuals to figure things out for themselves. It was also a period of great violence in which destructive weapons, made possible by new Iron Age technologies, encouraged rulers to expand their turf by warring against one another.[11]

The result was a profound social crisis in which old gods and old religions no longer provided satisfactory answers to new questions. Looking into their own hearts and minds, people felt the need for a leap in faith in what it means to be human. Prophetic voices began urging people to recognize a divinity and sacredness, both in themselves and in others, and to practice compassion by surrendering their egos. In each of these faiths the rejection of violence was linked to the practice of compassion.

Thus, all the great religions that emerged during the Axial Age include some form of the Golden Rule. For example, Confucius said that we should not act toward others as we would not want others to act toward us. In China the ideal ruler was no longer a warrior but someone whose deeds brought spiritual benefits to the people.

This new awakening to the divinity or sacredness within every human being is what Armstrong means by spirituality—a leap of faith, a practice of compassion based on a new belief in the sacredness of ourselves and other selves. We need to see the distinction between this concept of spirituality and what many practice as religion. Religion is belief in a body of ideas. Religious people, Armstrong argues, tend to be doctrinaire; they often prefer being right to being compassionate.

Armstrong is convinced that as a result of urbanization, globalization, and rapidly changing technology the whole world is now in the midst of a social crisis as profound as that of the Axial Age. We are therefore called on to make a similar leap in faith, to practice a similar compassion. Native People's view of the Earth as a sacred entity rather than only as a resource, she believes, provides us with a model.

To me, as a movement activist, this suggests that, to grapple with the interacting and seemingly intractable questions of today's society, we need to see ourselves not mainly as victims but as new men and women who, recognizing the sacredness in ourselves and in others, can view love and compassion, in the words of Martin Luther King Jr., not as "some sentimental and weak response" but instead as "the key that unlocks the door which leads to ultimate reality."[12]

TRANSFORMATIONAL ORGANIZING

The older I grow, the more I realize how lucky I am to have lived so long and been part of so many historic changes. When I became a radical nearly seventy years ago, we ran the "risk of seeming ridiculous," as Che Guevara put it, if we thought Love had anything to do with Revolution.[13]

Being revolutionary meant being tough as nails, committed to agitating and mobilizing angry and oppressed masses to overthrow the government and seize state power by any means necessary in order to reconstruct society from the top down.

In the past fifty years this top-down view of revolution has been discredited by the demise of the Soviet Union. At the same time our approach to revolution has been humanized by the modern women's movement, which informs us that the political is personal; the ecological movement, which emphasizes loving Mother Earth and the places where we live; and Martin Luther King Jr.'s call for a radical revolution in our values and his concept of "beloved community."

In the past fifteen years tens of thousands of very diverse community groups have sprung up all over the world to resist the commodifying by global corporations of our relationships to one another. On January 1, 1994, the day NAFTA took effect, the Zapatistas dramatized this new movement by first taking over six Mexican cities militarily and then retiring to Chiapas and other indigenous communities to engage the people at the grassroots in nonviolent struggles to create new forms of participatory democracy.

Nearly six years later, in the November 1999 "Battle of Seattle," fifty thousand members of labor, women, youth, and peace groups closed down the World Trade Organization to inform the world that the time has come to create alternatives to corporate globalization.

In 2001 a series of "Another World Is Possible" World Social Forums began in Porto Alegre, Brazil, to help movement activists around the world recognize that it is futile to keep calling on elected officials to create a more just, caring, and sustainable world. We ourselves must begin practicing in the social realm the capacity to care for each other, to share the food, skills, time, and ideas that up to now most of us have limited to our most cherished personal relationships.

As part and parcel of this new approach to revolution, the first United States Social Forum was held in Atlanta, Georgia, in 2007. The second inspired over eighteen thousand diverse activists to convene in Detroit in June 2010.

Normally it would take decades for a people to transform themselves from the hyperindividualist, hypermaterialist, damaged human beings that Americans in all walks of life are today to the loving, caring people we need in the deepening crises. But these are not normal times. If we don't speed up this transformation, the likelihood is that, armed with AK-47s, we will soon be at each other's throats.

That is why linking Love and Revolution is an idea whose time has come.

We urgently need to bring to our communities the limitless capacity to love, serve, and create for and with each other. We urgently need to bring the neighbor back into our hoods, not only in our inner cities but also in our suburbs, our gated communities, on Main Street and Wall Street, and on Ivy League campuses.

We are in the midst of a process that is nothing short of reinventing revolution. For much of the twentieth century the theory and practice of revolution have been dominated by overarching ideologies, purist paradigms, and absolutist views of a static Paradise; arguments over which class, race, or gender was the main revolutionary social force; and binary oppositions between Left and Right. Big victories have been prioritized over small collaborative actions that build community and neighborhoods: the end has been valued over the means. We rarely stopped to wonder how much this view of revolution reflected the capitalist culture that was dehumanizing us.

Now, in the light of our historical experiences and thanks especially to the indigenous cultures that the Zapatistas have revealed to us, we are beginning to understand that the world is always being made and never finished; that activism can be the journey rather than the arrival; that struggle doesn't always have to be confrontational but can take the form of reaching out to find common ground with the many "others" in our society who are also seeking ways out from alienation, isolation, privatization, and dehumanization by corporate globalization.

This is the kind of transformational organizing we need in this period. Instead of putting our organizational energies into begging Ford and General Motors to stay in Detroit—or begging the government to keep them afloat—so that they can continue to exploit us, we need to go beyond traditional capitalism. Creating new forms of community-based institutions (e.g., co-ops, small businesses, and community development corporations) will give us ownership and control over the way we make our living, while helping us to ensure that the well-being of the community and the environment is part of the bottom line.

Instead of buying all our food from the store, we need to be planting community and school gardens and creating farmers' markets that will not only provide us with healthier food but also enable us to raise our children in a nurturing relationship with the Earth.

Instead of trying to bully young people to remain in classrooms isolated from the community and structured to prepare them to become cogs in the existing economic system, we need to recognize that the reason why so many young people drop out from inner-city schools is because they are voting with their feet against an educational system that sorts, tracks, tests, and rejects or certifies them like products of a factory because it was created for the age of industrialization. They are crying out for another kind of education that gives them opportunities to exercise their creative energies because it values them as whole human beings.

This kind of organizing takes a lot of patience because changing people and people changing themselves requires time. Because it usually involves only small groups of people, it lacks the drama and visibility of angry masses making demands on the power structure. So it doesn't seem practical to those who think of change only in terms of quick fixes, huge masses, and charismatic leaders.

But as Margaret Wheatley puts it in *Leadership and the New Science*, we need a paradigm shift in our understanding of how change happens. "From a Newtonian perspective," Wheatley argues, "our efforts often seem too small, and we doubt that our actions will make a difference. Or perhaps we hope that our small efforts will contribute incrementally to large-scale change. Step by step, system by system, we aspire to develop enough mass or force to alter the larger system."

What the most advanced researchers and theoreticians in all of science now comprehend is that the Newtonian concept of a universe driven by mass force is out of touch with reality, for it fails to account for both observable phenomena and theoretical conundrums that can be explained only by quantum physics:

> A quantum view explains the success of small efforts quite differently. Acting locally allows us to be inside the movement and flow of the system, participating in all those complex events occurring simultaneously. We are more likely to be sensitive to the dynamics of this system, and thus more effective. However, changes in small places also affect the global system, not through incrementalism, but because every small system participates in an unbroken wholeness. Activities in one part of the whole create effects that appear in distant places. Because of these unseen connections, there is potential value in working anywhere in the system. We never know how our small activities will affect others through the invisible fabric of our connectedness.

In what Wheatley calls "this exquisitely connected world," the real engine of change is never "critical mass"; dramatic and systemic change always begins with "critical connections."[14]

So by now the crux of our preliminary needs should be apparent. We must open our hearts to new beacons of Hope. We must expand our minds to new modes of thought. We must equip our hands with new methods of organizing. And we must build on all of the humanity-stretching movements of the past half century: the Montgomery Bus Boycott; the civil rights movement; the Free Speech movement; the anti–Vietnam War movement; the Asian American, Native American, and Chicano movements; the women's movement; the gay and lesbian movement; the disability rights/pride movement; and the ecological and environmental justice movements. We must find ourselves amid the fifty million people who as activists or as supporters have engaged in the many-sided struggles to create the new democratic and life-affirming values that are needed to civilize U.S. society.

The transition to a better world is not guaranteed. We could destroy the planet, as those chanting "Drill, baby, drill!" seem determined to do. We could end up in barbarism unless we engage in and support positive struggles that create *more human* human beings and *more democratic* institutions. Our challenge, as we enter the third millennium, is to deepen the commonalities and the bonds between these tens of millions, while at the same time continuing to address the issues within our local communities by two-sided struggles that not only say "No" to the existing power structure but also empower our constituencies to embrace the power within each of us to create the world anew.

We must have the courage to walk the talk, but we must also engage in the continuing dialogues that enable us to break free of old categories and create the new ideas that are necessary to address our realities, because revolutions are made not to prove the correctness of ideas but to begin anew.

In this scenario everyone has a contribution to make, each according to our abilities, our energies, our experiences, our skills and where we are in our own lives. When I was much younger, I used to recite a poem that goes: "So much to do, so many to woo, and, oh, we are so very few." As I go around the country these days, making new friends and talking to people about the challenges of the new millennium, I still recognize that we have much to do and many to woo, but I no longer feel that we are so very few.

CHAPTER TWO

Revolution as a New Beginning

We are at a pivotal time in our country's history. The power structure is obviously unable to resolve the triple crises of global wars, global economic turmoil, and global warming. Millions are losing their jobs and homes. Workers feel they can no longer maintain the "American standard of living" that defined the "middle class." Barack Obama's "Yes, we can" call for change energized millions of young people, independents, and those fed up with Bush and the war. Now new sources of anger are being directed at Obama.

What we urgently need are impassioned discussions everywhere, in groups small and large, where people from all walks of life are not only talking but also listening to one another. That is the best way to begin creating an understanding of the next American Revolution, which I believe is not only the key to global survival but also the most important step we can take in this period to build a new, more human, more socially and ecologically responsible, and more secure nation that all of us, whatever our race, ethnicity, gender, faith, or national origin, will be proud to call our own.

What do we mean by revolution? It is hard to struggle for something that you have not yet tried to define and name. There is a popular sense of the term that we use to refer to everything from prominent historical events to dramatic sociocultural changes to the latest marketing trends. Newspaper columnists speak of the sexual revolution, the Internet revolution, and so on. Students are required to study the American Revolution and the industrial revolution.

Meanwhile, leftists, and many people who are not leftists, have tended to hold onto the concept of revolution created in the early twentieth century that involves the seizure of state power by a party representing the working class or "the oppressed masses." Those leftists who pride themselves on being "revolutionary" have usually sought to distinguish themselves from liberals and social democrats who are "reformists" and lack the will or chutzpah necessary to seize state power and bring about wholesale societal changes.

That is why those of us who are serious about transforming our society—socially, culturally, and politically—need to clarify what we mean by "revolution." We especially need to explain how and why the ideas of most leftists about revolution have become narrow, static, and even counterrevolutionary.

The historian I have found to be most insightful about the rethinking of radical strategies mandated by the movements of the 1960s is Immanuel Wallerstein, author of *The Modern World-System: Capitalist Agriculture and the Origins of the European World-Economy in the Sixteenth Century.* In my copy of the book I have kept the review that was published on the front page of the Sunday *New York Times* book review section more than thirty years ago.[1]

The movements of the 1960s, writes Wallerstein in *After Liberalism,* published in 1995, culminated in what he calls "the world revolution of 1968." Since that world revolution, he says, six premises that were accepted as axiomatic by revolutionaries since the French Revolution have become questionable:

- The two-step strategy (first take state power, then transform society) is no longer self-evidently correct.
- We can no longer assume that political activity is most effective if channeled through one party.
- The labor-capital conflict is not the only fundamental conflict in capitalism; there are also contradictions revolving around gender, race, ethnicity, and sexuality.
- Democracy is not a bourgeois concept but a profoundly revolutionary, anticapitalist idea.
- An increase in productivity is not an essential goal of socialism. We need to address capitalism's ecological and human consequences, including consumerism and the commodification of everything.
- We need to reassess our faith in science and reconsider the complex relationships between determinism and free will and between order and chaos.[2]

Next, in his little 1998 book, *Utopistics: Or, Historical Choices of the Twenty-First Century,* Wallerstein explains how 1968 dethroned both the Leninists and the Social Democrats, the two antisystemic movements that had emerged from and prevailed since the French Revolution. After 1968 people the world over, including in Africa and Asia, no longer believed in the ability of state structures to improve the commonweal. This "resulted in a kind of widespread and amorphous antistatism, of a kind totally unknown in the long period between 1789 and 1968. It was debilitating and aroused fear as well as uncertainty."[3]

The next year, in *The End of the World as We Know It: Social Science for the Twenty-First Century,* Wallerstein assured us that uncertainty rather than certainty about the future provides the basis for hope.[4] In 2001 I had a warm discussion with Wallerstein at Binghamton University. Since then we have been on each other's mailing list. When I turned ninety in 2005, he e-mailed me that he was coming to Detroit for my hundredth birthday. To my delight, he instead came to Detroit in 2010 to celebrate my ninety-fifth birthday and to engage in a spirited conversation on the meaning of revolution at the United States Social Forum. Bloggers and online activists made audio and video recordings of our conversation, which can be found all over the Web.

Wallerstein's work has particularly resonated with me because I have come to similar conclusions as a result of my movement experiences. After I came to Detroit fifty-seven years ago and became involved in and committed to real and ongoing community struggles, I began to understand why so many leftist ideas of revolution have nothing to do with the actual process by which real human beings, confronted with real and seemingly intractable problems, make decisions and exercise their capacities to create new ways of living. Their choices become a new beginning in the continuing evolution of human beings toward becoming more creative, conscious, self-critical, and politically and socially responsible.

By contrast, many leftists cling to a nineteenth-century ideology that forecasts the future. Then they view everything that happens as a sort of validation of what they think. That was very much the way most of us in the radical movements thought for much of the twentieth century.

I began my movement activism in the early 1940s when, in the wake of the Great Depression and the sit-down strikes waged by millions of factory and office workers all over the country, the writings of public intellectuals and academicians began to reflect the influence of Karl Marx's ideas of class and class struggle.[5]

Having been born female and Chinese American, I had known from early on that changes were needed in our society, but not until I left the university in 1940 with a PhD in philosophy did it occur to me that I might be involved in making those changes. At that point, confronted with the need to make a living, I realized how unlikely it was that I would ever do so as a university professor. In those days, before the movements of the sixties, even department stores would come right out and say "we don't hire Orientals."

Luckily for me, my personal crisis coincided with the beginning of World War II and the emergence of the March on Washington movement, led by A. Philip Randolph, demanding jobs for blacks in the defense plants. A precursor of the modern civil rights movement, this mass campaign pushed FDR to issue Executive Order 8802, which created the Fair Employment Practices Committee and outlawed discrimination in factories receiving contracts from the government for war-related production. As a result, tens of thousands of blacks who had toiled under the oppressive conditions of the Jim Crow South migrated to Detroit and cities throughout the Midwest, Northeast, and West Coast for a chance to work in the factory jobs that opened up during the war.

I became involved with this movement and was so inspired by its success that I decided that what I wanted to do with the rest of my life was become a movement activist in the black community. Toward that goal I joined the Workers Party, which through the South Side Tenants Organization had brought me into contact with the black community.

The Workers Party was a Trotskyist organization, but I never considered myself a Trotskyite. By the time I came on the political scene in 1940 at the beginning of World War II, the controversy over why the Russian Revolution in 1917 had not lived up to its promise was no longer at the center of world politics. I have learned over the years that *when* you become a radical usually decides your politics.

During the 1920s and 1930s, in the wake of the Russian Revolution, radicals all over the world split into rival camps, reflecting the split between Trotsky and Stalin that had occurred in the Soviet Union following Lenin's death. After Stalin rose to power, he pushed forward with aggressive industrialization and modernization plans while using repressive measures to curtail his political opposition. While the Soviet Union under Stalin became a leading force of revolutionary and socialist parties internationally, his political foes and other critics struggled to understand why a revolution made in the name of proletarian rule had led to Stalin's gulags. Huge ideological and physical battles were waged between Stalinists and Trotskyists, each convinced that they had the truth.

I was fortunate that, mostly by accident, I wound up with the anti-Stalinists, to which the Trotskyites belonged. (Because they were generally in the minority—and thus on the receiving end of Stalin's repression and censorship—the anti-Stalinists upheld more democratic standards of debate and practice that tempered Stalinist notions of dictatorship and centralized authority.) But, whether Stalinist or anti-Stalinist, radicals in the United States and the world—remember this is well before the age of the Internet or even television—were unable to analyze the events in Russia as anything more than abstractions. As a result, those whose politics were formed in that period tended to be students or intellectuals deeply invested in their "line struggles" (i.e., fierce battles over political positions) with their leftist adversaries.

By contrast, after nearly twenty years in classrooms, I came to the movement on the wave of growing black militancy at the beginning of World War II and joined the Workers Party because I was primarily interested in getting my feet wet in practical activities. Even though I was leaving the academy behind, I still viewed myself as an intellectual who, having studied Hegel (the German philosopher of the late eighteenth and early nineteenth centuries), was acutely aware of the power of ideas to be both liberating and limiting.

From Hegel I had gained an appreciation of how we as human beings have evolved over many thousands of years, struggling for Freedom (or what we today call "self-determination"). Constantly striving to overcome the contradictions or negatives that inevitably arise in the course of struggle, constantly challenged to break free from views that were at one time liberating but had become fetters because reality had changed, we are required to create new ideas that make more concrete and more universal our concept of what it means to be free. These notions lie at the core of a Hegelian method of dialectical thinking.

In my last year of graduate work I had also been drawn to the American pragmatists George Herbert Mead and John Dewey, who helped me to unthink the sharp separation between the True and the Good that was entrenched in Western thought and to recognize that individuals can develop to their human potential only through their involvement in community.[6]

That is why inside the Workers Party I was immediately attracted to the Johnson-Forest Tendency led by C. L. R. James, the West Indian historian (best known for his book *The Black Jacobins,* on the Haitian Revolution), and Raya Dunayevskaya, a Russian-born self-educated intellectual who had once been Trotsky's secretary.[7] The "Johnsonites," as they were known, appealed to me in the first place because, unlike most radicals in that period, they emphasized the significance of the independent "Negro" struggle in the making of an American Revolution. They were also avid students of Hegel. So their Marxism and Leninism were very different from that of most who called themselves Marxist-Leninists. Instead of being economist and determinist, their Marxism was humanist. Instead of focusing on Lenin's strategies for the seizure of power, they emphasized his profoundly democratic vision that "every cook can govern." Challenging the view held by most radicals that they were building the vanguard party needed to lead the masses to play some historically prescribed role, they celebrated and encouraged the self-activity and self-organization of workers and marginalized people, seeing them as the force to bring about real social change.

Discovering Marxism as a Johnsonite was as empowering and liberating as my discovery of Hegel—or his Enlightenment predecessor, Kant—had been in the university. Together we spent hours studying and discussing each of the great revolutions of the past, focusing not so much on the oppression suffered by people at the bottom of the society but on how they organized themselves and in the process advanced the whole society. The important thing for us was to see the oppressed not mainly as victims or objects but as creative subjects. To reinforce this view, we went back to the early Marx, the young man who in 1843 at the age of twenty-four and as a student of Hegel had written the *Economic and Philosophic Manuscripts,* emphasizing the human essence of the workers and their alienation in capitalist society.[8]

Through our immersion in the writings of the early Marx, we developed a very different view of capitalism and socialism from that accepted by traditional Marxists. Being a Marxist for us meant focusing not on property relationships but on the spiritual as well as the physical misery of capitalism. Capitalism, we argued, reduces the workers to a fragment, robbing them of their natural and acquired powers. It alienates them from their species and communal essence. Socialism, by contrast, means the reappropriation by the oppressed of their human and social essence.

Hence, in our view, Marx's materialism was not the materialism of consumerism. It was the materialism of rooting ideas in real life and practice, going beyond talk and ideas alone. For example, Marx criticized Hegel for grappling only with theoretical labor and neglecting practical, life-sustaining labor. And he criticized the philosopher Ludwig Feuerbach for rooting ideas too much in Nature and not enough in practice and in politics. When you read Marx (or Jesus) this way, you come to see that real wealth is not material wealth and real poverty is not just the lack of food, shelter, and clothing. Real poverty is the belief that the purpose of life is acquiring wealth and owning things. Real wealth is not the possession of property but the recognition that our deepest need, as human beings, is to keep developing our natural and acquired powers and to relate to other human beings.

In the 1940s there was very little appreciation or understanding of this side of Marx. Every Marxist-Leninist owned and referred to the *Communist Manifesto*, just as the Black Panthers and young people in the 1960s carried around Mao's *Red Book*. By contrast, as a Johnsonite, I appreciated the *Manifesto* as a historical work rather than a timeless road map. My favorite passage in the *Communist Manifesto* comes at the end of that fantastic paragraph that begins with "the bourgeoisie cannot exist without constantly revolutionizing the instruments of production" and ends with "All that is solid melts into air, all that is holy is profaned, and man is at last compelled to face with sober senses, his real conditions of life, and his relations with his kind."[9]

This focus on the human and spiritual contradictions that arise from revolutionizing technology is very different than the stage theory of history, from feudalism to capitalism to communism, which most radicals back then took from the *Manifesto*. It is very different from the kind of writing that most people associate with Marx.

I often remind people that Marx was born in 1818, one year before *Moby Dick* author Herman Melville, and that he wrote the *Manifesto* when he was twenty-nine. I became a radical when I was twenty-five. When you are twenty-five or twenty-nine, especially if you are an intellectual, you see your world and make leaps in ideas in a particular way. In the unions that were then being formed, Marx saw a new kind of community being created and expanded that perception into the great vision of *communism* that inspired millions of people all around the world. Over the years I have found it helpful to remember Marx's age and where he was coming from when he was writing the *Manifesto*. He had recently come from years of studying Hegel and was imbued with Hegel's tremendous sense of historical sweep, the vision of the universal becoming constantly more concrete, and the concrete constantly becoming more universal. It is a wonderful way of thinking, but it also tends to get to the absolute like a shot out of a pistol, as Hegel put it, without "the suffering, the patience, and the labour of the negative."[10]

Marx was writing in the British Museum; he was not experiencing all the contradictions that emerge in reality. I remember falling in love with what Marx said about the Paris Commune being "the political form at last discovered under which to work out the economic emancipation of labor."[11] It opened up my mind. But since then I have recognized that the Paris Commune emerged more than a hundred years ago in a war between the French and the Germans. It is not impossible that something like the Paris Commune will emerge out of the Iraq War, but to think that it will assume the same form in the twenty-first century is a kind of thinking that we should rid ourselves of. It involves taking a model that happened in historical reality many years ago and gauging perspectives for the future on that model when reality is always changing.

These two notions—that reality is constantly changing and that you must constantly be aware of the new and more challenging contradictions that drive change—lie at the core of dialectical thinking. In graduate school at Bryn Mawr, the philosophies of Kant and Hegel had given meaning to my personal life. But it was not until I became a Johnsonite, studying the revolutions of the past and trying to make an American Revolution in the present, that I began to understand the critical importance of dialectical thinking to movement activists and freedom fighters.

Hegel's method of thinking dialectically did not just come out of his head. He began to think dialectically because he was trying to make sense of the contradictory developments in his reality. As a young man, he had hailed the French Revolution by dancing around the tree of liberty. Twenty years later Napoleon was in power. On the one hand, the revolution was obviously a great leap forward for Humankind because it overthrew the feudal aristocracy and brought the great masses of the French people into the public arena as active citizens making the social decisions that had previously been the prerogative of the upper classes. On the other hand, the French Revolution had also led to the Napoleonic dictatorship; it had opened the road for the rapid development of capitalism, which robbed workers of their skills and reduced them to appendages of machines. As a result, a lot of people in intellectual circles began wondering whether the French Revolution had been worth making and some of them even began advocating a return to the good old feudal days. Hegel could have given up on Humanity or on the struggle for Freedom. Instead, he created a method of thinking, a philosophy, that encourages the freedom fighter to view the contradictions that emerge in the course of every struggle as a challenge to take Humanity to a higher plateau by creating a new ideal, a new, more concrete universal vision of Freedom.

That is why the study of Hegel was so important to Lenin in 1915 when the German Social Democrats supported their own government in World War I, abandoning the position of international solidarity of the working class on which the Second International had been founded. Their betrayal forced Lenin to recognize that capitalism had reached a new stage, the stage of imperialism and monopolies. As the Western industrial nations ravaged the world, workers in the West indirectly enjoyed the spoils of colonialism. The German Social Democrats and the Second International became a part of what Lenin called the labor aristocracy, more intent on maintaining the privileges of living in an imperialist nation than building the international socialist movement to challenge imperialism. He therefore concluded that there was a need to create a new revolutionary movement and a new International. Basing his ideas on the Soviet thought that had emerged in the Russian Revolution of 1905 and that incorporated a much higher stage of self-activity and self-organization than the unions, Lenin was able to create a new vision of *socialism* as a society in which "every cook can govern."

I spent ten years in New York working closely with C. L. R. James and Raya Dunayevskaya, while also learning the nuts and bolts of radical organizing by doing the work of a party member. But I was delighted when the Johnsonites came to the conclusion in 1951 that both the Workers Party and the Socialist Workers Party (another Trotskyist group that the Johnsonites briefly aligned with) were too stuck in the ideas they had derived mainly from the Russian Revolution to recognize the new social forces for an American Revolution—blacks, women, rank-and-file workers, and youth—that had emerged out of the socializing experiences of World War II. So we decided to set out on our own to launch an independent newspaper called *Correspondence* that would be written and edited by representatives of these new social forces and published in Detroit.

That is why I moved to Detroit in 1953 and soon thereafter married Jimmy Boggs.

Living and working with Jimmy in the black community of Detroit I began to see the relationship between ideas and historical reality in a completely different light. C. L. R. and Raya were both powerful intellectuals, and I had learned a lot from working with them. But their ideas about workers had come more from books and from struggles with other radicals whose ideas about workers also came from books than out of real-life struggles. The Johnsonite mantra had been the famous paragraph in *Capital* where Marx celebrates "the revolt of the working-class, a class always increasing in numbers and disciplined, united, organised by the very mechanism of the process of capitalist production itself."[12] In other words, despite all our efforts to learn from people at the grassroots, we had still not completely broken with the view of "the masses" as an abstraction created by history rather than as the creators of new beginnings.

Jimmy was a breath of fresh air. He was an organic intellectual, someone whose ideas came not out of books but mainly from reflecting on the experiences of his own life and those of his "kind." Born in Marion Junction, Alabama, a tiny country town with two stores on its main street, he had moved to Detroit after graduating from high school. Working on the line at Chrysler Jefferson (a huge plant on the Eastside of Detroit), he became a rank-and-file militant, absorbing from the left-wing forces in the United Auto Workers (which union leader Walter Reuther had not yet red-baited out of the union) the fundamental concepts of class, race, and socialism that helped him to see himself as a continuation of thousands of years of human struggle to be free and self-determining. After World War II he experienced the decimation of the workforce by automation. As a result, he was very conscious of the tremendous changes taking place in his reality *and* conscious of his own identity as a worker who had lived through three epochs of human struggle to extend our material powers: agriculture, industry, and automation. Because he had this dialectical sense of constantly changing reality and of himself as a historical person, he also had the audacity, the chutz-pah, to recognize—as he did in his book *The American Revolution: Pages from a Negro Worker's Notebook*—that Marx's ideas, created in a period of material scarcity, could no longer guide us in our period of material abundance and that it was now up to him to do for our period what Marx had done for his.

When I began living in Detroit in 1953, Jimmy, a member of the United Auto Workers, was still mainly engaged with his fellow workers in struggles in the plant against automation and speed-ups (which workers in the plant called "man-o-mation"). But by the 1960s he had concluded that because unions were unable or unwilling to struggle with management over the fundamental questions raised by Hi-Tech, the workplace was no longer the main site of struggle, and revolutionaries should focus instead on the profoundly new questions about how to live and make a living that were being asked by the "Outsiders" in the community, who in Detroit were mainly young black people. As he put it in *The American Revolution*, "Thus, at this point in American history when the labor movement is on the decline [because it can't solve the issues raised by Hi-Tech], the Negro movement is on the upsurge."[13]

During the 1950s I mainly listened and learned from being with Jimmy in the many meetings he held with workers from his plant and with people in the community. However, by the 1960s I felt I had been living in the black community long enough to play an active role in the Black Power movement that was emerging organically in a Detroit where blacks were becoming the majority. So while Jimmy wrote articles and made speeches challenging Black Power militants to face the questions of Hi-Tech, I was doing a lot of organizing in the Black Power movement. In the next chapter, I discuss this work in greater detail. What I want to note here is how the explosion of the Detroit Rebellion in July 1967 and the meteoric rise of the Black Panther Party in the late 1960s forced us to pause and rethink the Marxist-Leninist ideas about revolution that leftists had long accepted as self-evident.

In 1967 Jimmy and I had each been in the radical movement for more than twenty years, but we had never felt compelled to address head-on the questions of what is a revolution and how do you make it. Then, with rebellions breaking out all over and young blacks joining the Black Panther Party by the tens of thousands, we had to ask ourselves whether there is a fundamental distinction between a rebellion and a revolution. Out of that questioning, we concluded that although rebellion is a stage in the development of revolution, it falls far short of revolution. As we wrote in *Revolution and Evolution in the Twentieth Century,* rebellions are important because they represent the standing up of the oppressed. Rebellions break the threads that have been holding the system together. They shake up old values so that relations between individuals and groups within society are unlikely ever to be the same again. But rebels see themselves and call on others to see them mainly as victims. They do not see themselves as responsible for reorganizing society, which is what the revolutionary social forces must do in a revolutionary period. They are not prepared to create the foundation for a new society. Thus, while a rebellion usually begins with the belief on the part of the oppressed that they can change things from the way they are to the way they should be, they usually end by saying, "*They* ought to do this and *they* ought to do that." In other words, because rebellions do not go beyond protesting injustices, they increase the dependency rather than the self-determination of the oppressed.[14]

We also recognized that those who purport to be revolutionaries but deny or evade this lesson of history and continue to celebrate or encourage rebellions do so mainly because they view themselves as the leaders of angry and oppressed but essentially faceless masses. If or when they gain power, they may make some reforms, but they are powerless to make fundamental changes because they have not empowered the oppressed prior to taking power.

In the Black Panther Party and the rebellions of the 1960s, there was a lot of righteous anger because in the sixties we defined ourselves more by our oppression than by the power that we have within us to create new loving relationships. That is why, beginning in 1968, Jimmy and I felt that our main responsibility as revolutionaries was to go beyond "protest politics," beyond just increasing the anger and outrage of the oppressed, and concentrate instead on projecting and initiating struggles that involve people at the grassroots in assuming the responsibility for creating the new values, truths, infrastructures, and institutions that are necessary to build and govern a new society.

Now that the rebellions of the late sixties had broken the threads that have been holding the system together, we said, now that urban rebellions had become part of the U.S. political landscape, now that the constant revolutionizing of production had created everlasting uncertainty and compelled people in all layers of society to face with sober senses our conditions of life and our relations with our kind, now that capitalism had defiled all our human relationships by turning them into money relationships, revolutionaries urgently need to project new ideas and new forms of struggles. Activists transform and empower themselves when they struggle to change their reality by exploring, in theory and practice, the potentially revolutionary social forces of Work, Education, Community, Citizenship, Patriotism, Health, Justice, and Democracy.

At a time when so many radicals in the United States were saying and thinking "I hate this lousy country" and looking all over the world for models of revolution—China, Southeast Asia, Africa, Latin America, even tiny countries such as Albania that were nothing like the United States—Jimmy and I also set out to understand in a deeper manner what was exceptional about U.S. history and therefore what would distinguish the next American Revolution from revolutions in other times and other countries. In struggling to understand the uniqueness of our history, our goal differed sharply from the nation's mythology that hails the United States and its citizenry as uniquely free and democratic and thus destined to remake the world in its own image. (This is the type of American exceptionalism that drove Bush and the neocons not only to invade Iraq but also to arrogantly and falsely believe that the Iraqi people and the rest of the world would hail them as liberators rather than occupiers.) But we knew that an endless rebellion against America would lead nowhere. So even as we actively opposed U.S. imperialism, we sought to build on the revolutionary beginnings of this country and the many struggles to build "a more perfect union" that have taken place over the past two hundred years. At the same time, by recognizing the counterrevolutionary tendencies and forces stemming from the pursuit of rapid economic growth that had been built in its founding, we were also able to recognize our need and responsibility to transform ourselves and our institutions.

In 1968 Jimmy and I started Conversations in Maine with our old friends and comrades Freddy and Lyman Paine to explore how a revolution in our time and in our country would differ from the many revolutions that had taken place around the world in the early to mid-twentieth century. Together, we brought vastly different life experiences to the table that also reflected the diversity of this country: Jimmy was a black autoworker born in the Jim Crow South; Lyman, a Harvard-educated Boston Brahmin; Freddy, a Jewish immigrant who got into activism as a young worker; and myself, an Asian American woman with a PhD. All of us had been Johnsonites, but C. L. R. James had disowned us in 1962 when we insisted that the shrinking of the working class by automation demanded that we revisit some of the foundational concepts of Marxism.

Our separation freed us to recognize unequivocally that we were coming to the end of the relatively short industrial epoch on which Marx's epic analysis had been based. We could see clearly that the United States was in the process of transitioning to a new mode of production based on new information technologies; that this transitioning was not only ending but also liberating us from the industrial epoch that had alienated us from the Earth and from each other; and therefore that its cultural and political ramifications are as far-reaching as those involved in the transition from hunting and gathering to agriculture or from agriculture to industry.

Thus, as movement activists and theoreticians in the tumultuous year of 1968, we were also acutely conscious that in the wake of the civil rights movement—beginning with the Montgomery Bus Boycott in 1955, the rise of ecological awareness, and the exploding anti–Vietnam War and women's movements—new and more profound questions of our relationships with one another, with Nature, and with other countries were being raised with a centrality unthinkable in earlier revolutions.

As our conversations continued, we became increasingly convinced that our revolution in our country in the late twentieth century had to be radically different from the revolutions that had taken place in pre- or nonindustrialized countries such as Russia, Cuba, China, or Vietnam. Those revolutions had been made not only to correct injustices but also to achieve rapid economic growth. By contrast, as citizens of a nation that had achieved its rapid economic growth and prosperity at the expense of African Americans, Native Americans, other people of color, and peoples all over the world, our priority had to be in correcting the injustices and backwardness of our relationships with one another, with other countries, and with the Earth.

In other words, our revolution had to be for the purpose of accelerating our evolution to a higher plateau of Humanity. That's why we called our philosophy "dialectical humanism" as contrasted with the "dialectical materialism" of Marxist-Leninists. Six years later, nearly thirty years before 9/11, the practical implications of this somewhat abstract concept of an American Revolution were spelled out by Jimmy in the chapter titled "Dialectics and Revolution" in *Revolution and Evolution in the Twentieth Century:*

> The revolution to be made in the United States will be the first revolution in history to require the masses to make material sacrifices rather than to acquire more material things. We must give up many of the things which this country has enjoyed at the expense of damning over one-third of the world into a state of underdevelopment, ignorance, disease, and early death. . . . [Until then] this country will not be safe for the world and revolutionary warfare on an international scale against the United States will remain the wave of the present. . . . It is obviously going to take a tremendous transformation to prepare the people of the United States for these new social goals. But potential revolutionaries can only become true revolutionaries if they take the side of those who believe that humanity can be transformed.[15]

Thirty years ago when many young people were studying this book in small groups in the aftermath of the struggles of the sixties, I doubt that they paid much attention to this paragraph. But with the economic meltdown and global warming, and especially since 9/11, this projection demands our most serious discussion. We have obviously reached a turning point not only in the history of the human race but also in the history of Planet Earth. Scientists believe that the dinosaurs were extinguished by a meteor sixty-five million years ago, an external cause. If in this period we, and all living beings on our planet, are extinguished, it will not be by an external cause. It will be because of the extravagant, thoughtless ways that we have been getting and spending and seeing little in Nature that is ours. Our challenge is to recognize our responsibility for the economic meltdown and the planetary emergency and transform our way of life accordingly. When we do, we will reach a new plateau in our continuing evolution as human beings.

The next American Revolution, at this stage in our history, is not principally about jobs or health insurance or making it possible for more people to realize the American Dream of upward mobility. It is about acknowledging that we Americans have enjoyed middle-class comforts at the expense of other peoples all over the world. It is about living the kind of lives that will not only slow down global warming but also end the galloping inequality both inside this country and between the Global North and the Global South. It is about creating a new American Dream whose goal is a higher Humanity instead of the higher standard of living dependent on Empire. It is about practicing a new, more active, global, and participatory concept of citizenship. It is about becoming the change we wish to see in the world.

The courage, commitment, and strategies required for this kind of revolution are very different from those required to storm the Winter Palace or the White House. Instead of viewing the U.S. people as masses to be mobilized in increasingly aggressive struggles for higher wages, better jobs, or guaranteed health care, we must have the courage to challenge ourselves to engage in activities that build a new and better world by improving the physical, psychological, political, and spiritual health of ourselves, our families, our communities, our cities, our world, and our planet.

This means that it is not enough to organize mobilizations that call on Congress and the president to end the wars in Iraq and Afghanistan. We must also challenge the American people to examine why 9/11 happened and why so many people around the world understand, even though they do not support the terrorists, that they were driven to these acts by frustration and anger at the U.S. role in the world, such as supporting the Israeli occupation of Palestine and dictatorships in the Middle East and treating whole countries, the peoples of the world, and Nature only as resources enabling us to maintain our middle-class way of life.

We have to help the American people find the moral strength to recognize that—although no amount of money can compensate for the countless deaths and indescribable suffering that our criminal invasion and occupation have caused the Iraqi people—we, the American people, have a responsibility to make the material sacrifices that will enable them to begin rebuilding their infrastructure. We have to help the American people grow their souls enough to recognize that because we have been consuming 25 percent of the planet's fossil fuels even though we are less than 5 percent of the world's population, we are the ones who must take the first big steps to reduce greenhouse emissions. We are the ones who must begin to live more simply so that others can simply live.

Moreover, we urgently need to begin creating ways to live more frugally and more cooperatively NOW because with times getting harder, we can easily slip into scapegoating "the other" and goose-stepping behind a nationalist leader, as the good Germans did in the 1930s.

This vision of an American Revolution as Transformation is the one projected by Dr. Martin Luther King Jr. in his groundbreaking anti–Vietnam War speech on April 4, 1967. As Vincent Harding, Martin's close friend and colleague, has pointed out,

King was calling on us to redeem the soul of America. Speaking for the weak, the poor, the despairing, and the alienated, in our inner cities and in the rice paddies of Vietnam, he was urging us to become a more mature people by making a radical revolution not only against racism but also against materialism and militarism. He was challenging us to "rededicate ourselves to the long and bitter, but beautiful, struggle for a new world."[16]

King was assassinated before he could devise concrete ways to move us toward this radical revolution of values. The question we need to struggle over is "why haven't we who think of ourselves as American radicals picked up the torch?" Is it because a radical revolution of values against racism, materialism, and militarism is beyond our imagination, even though we are citizens of a nation with seven hundred military bases, whose unbridled consumerism imperils the planet?

In Detroit we are engaged in this long and beautiful struggle for a new world because we have learned through our own experience that just changing the color of those in political power was not enough to stem the devastation of our city resulting from deindustrialization. Our City of Hope campaign involves rebuilding, redefining, and respiriting Detroit from the ground up: growing food on abandoned lots, reinventing education to include children in community building, creating co-operatives to produce local goods for local needs, developing Peace Zones to transform our relationships with one another in our homes and on our streets, and replacing a punitive justice system with restorative justice programs to keep nonviolent offenders in our communities and out of multibillion-dollar prisons that not only misspend monies much needed for roads and schools but also turn minor offenders into hardened criminals.

It is a multigenerational campaign, involving the very old as well as the very young, and all the in-betweens, especially those born in the 1980s millennial generation whose aptitude with the new communications technology empowers them to be remarkably self-inventive and multitasking and to connect and reconnect 24/7 with individuals near and far.

Over the past two decades, people have been coming from all over the United States and the world to study what we are doing. I often sum it up by calling Detroit the Chiapas of North America. Despite the huge difference in local conditions, our Detroit–City of Hope campaign has more in common with the revolutionary struggles of the Zapatistas in Chiapas than with the Russian Revolution of 1917.[17]

People come from all over the world to learn from the Zapatista movement, initiated in 1994 by the Indigenous Peoples of Chiapas, because it is a movement based on thinking dialectically about War and Revolution. In the twentieth century, the Zapatistas explain, we lived through three world wars: World War I, World War II, and the cold war between the United States and the Soviet Union. All three were wars between nation-states or allied powers for control of discrete territories around the globe. All three had identifiable fronts. All three took place before the onset of globalization and the establishment of corporate rule over the world.

Therefore, World War IV, the war in which the whole world is now engaged, is a new kind of war: an ongoing and total war, the war of the "Empire of Money" against Humanity. The Empire of Money seeks to impose the logic and practice of capital on everything, to turn every living being, the Earth, our communities, and all our human relationships into commodities to be bought and sold on the market. It seeks to destroy everything that human beings have created: cultures, languages, memories, ideas, dreams, love, and respect for one another. It even destroys the material basis for the nation-state that Western societies created in the nineteenth century to protect us, if only marginally, from the forces of money.

Under these historically new conditions the meaning of revolution must also undergo a dialectical change. Fighting on the side of Humanity against the Empire of Money, we need to go beyond opposition, beyond rebellion, beyond resistance, beyond civic insurrection. We don't want to be like them. We don't want to become the "political class," to simply change presidents and switch governments.

We want and need to create the other alternative world that is now both possible and necessary. We want and need to exercise power, not take it.

The revolutionary organizing that the Zapatistas have been doing since 1994 flows from this new meaning of revolution. Their struggles are very local. They encourage communities to exercise power by developing their own projects to produce food and clothing and other supplies, solving their own problems of health and education, making their own decisions and in the process slowly but surely developing themselves. By recuperating traditional customs and practices for choosing governance democratically, resolving problems through dialogue and consensus, and rotating positions and responsibilities to prevent corruption, the Zapatistas have developed a new generation that has grown up with alternative, autonomous education and health programs and has begun to hold delegated positions in the autonomous municipalities.

We cannot use the Zapatista model as a blueprint for struggle in the United States because our history and our contemporary conditions are qualitatively different. What the Zapatistas demonstrate, however, is the need for a paradigm shift in our thinking. This term was introduced by Thomas S. Kuhn in his 1962 classic, *The Structure of Scientific Revolutions.* A paradigm shift, he said, is the totally new perspective needed at turning points in history when a prevailing concept fails to explain recurring phenomena. An example is the sixteenth-century recognition that the Earth is not the center of the universe, known as the Copernican Revolution.[18]

Our circular debates in the United States about our mounting social crises illustrate the need for such a paradigm shift. Millions of Americans, out of concern for their own families or for others less fortunate, are worried about our failing health and education systems. Thus, we have been locked in a titanic battle between the Left and the Right over the proper role of government and the redistribution of resources from the haves to the have-nots. This is a battle whose outcome carries significant implications for all Americans. The problem is that our debate is confined to narrow parameters. Too often we regard health care and education as commodities, and we remain complicit as our elected representatives reduce us to consumers. We forgo an opportunity to debate and discuss real solutions to the crises at hand. Instead of focusing directly on the issue of health *care,* our political discourse centers on health *insurance* programs that have more to do with feeding the already monstrous medical-industrial complex than with our physical, mental, and spiritual health.

Once we understand that our schools are in such crisis because they were created a hundred years ago in the industrial epoch to prepare children to become cogs in the economic machine, once we recognize that our challenge in the twenty-first century is to engage our children from K–12 in problem-solving and community-building activities, children and young people will become participants in caring for their own health and that of their families and communities. By eating food they have grown for themselves instead of obesity- and diabetes-producing fast foods, by creating and sharing information from the Internet, and by organizing health festivals for the community, they will not only be caring for their own health but also helping to heal our communities.

Or, as I often put it, "We have the power within us to create the world anew." We need to see that we can solve our health and education problems only by first creating a new concept of citizenship—one that will also cure our failing political system. That is what the next American Revolution is about.

CHAPTER THREE

Let's Talk about Malcolm and Martin

History is not the past. It is the stories we tell about the past. *How* we tell these stories—triumphantly or self-critically, metaphysically or dialectically—has a lot to do with whether we cut short or advance our evolution as human beings.

Historians of the black experience have a crucial role to play in helping blacks and everyone in this country develop a common understanding of the important role that the black struggle for human rights has played through the years not only to advance blacks but also to humanize this country. We need to revisit the movements of the sixties. But we cannot just celebrate the victories. We need to examine the new challenges and contradictions that emerged in the course of the struggle.

What lessons can we learn from these new contradictions? To know where we're going as a new movement is emerging, we need to know where we've been. What did we accomplish by the civil rights and Black Power struggles of the 1960s and 1970s, and what new contradictions did we create for ourselves and for the country?

It has been my experience that in the excitement of an emerging movement, we tend to want to be part of the action, and we underestimate the power and importance of the ideas in our heads and hearts. Movement activists today, whatever our class or race, cannot grapple with the challenges of the next American Revolution unless we make a serious effort to understand the lives and works of Malcolm X and Martin Luther King Jr.

For many Americans, including movement activists, Malcolm remains what he was in the 1960s, an icon of militancy and rebellion. Those who came of age in the era of Black Power still revere Malcolm and can recite his most memorable quotes. In the 1980s and 1990s members of the hip-hop generation began to claim Malcolm as one of their own. Sparked in part by the popularization of Malcolm through Spike Lee's biographical feature film, millions of young people read *The Autobiography of Malcolm X,* bought posters, and donned "X" caps and T-shirts featuring Malcolm in his signature black spectacles. Because he remains a symbol of Black Power in the popular American psyche—alongside Stokely Carmichael, Angela Davis, and the Black Panthers—Malcolm is still viewed as a polarizing figure by many white Americans, who mainly recall his fist raising and anti-white rhetoric during his years with the Nation of Islam.

Malcolm's life, however, was driven by a series of transformations. To freeze him in time as an anti-white orator and organizer for the Nation of Islam is to miss the central theme of his autobiography: the continuing reflection and transformations that he and all revolutionaries need to undergo as reality changes.

In contrast to Malcolm X, King has become, at least on the surface, an icon of American unity. The King holiday is treasured as a day that brings all people together regardless of

race, religion, class, gender, or partisan affiliation, a day to celebrate the diversity that makes America strong and proud. Most
Americans celebrate King primarily for his "I Have a Dream"
speech delivered at the 1963 March on Washington. They regard
him as a positive figure who worked with whites to help the
United States overcome the problems of bigotry and segregation
that served as the nation's principal obstacles to progress. This
rosy recasting of King's life and struggles also distorts history. It
erases from view both the real hostility with which his ideas and
actions were greeted and the profound changes in his views as
he wrestled in the last three years of his life with the challenges
of the Vietnam War and the urban rebellions.

Although the civil rights movement drew thousands of white
participants and allies, there were millions of white Americans
who perceived King as a polarizing figure. Such negative perceptions of King were not limited to Southerners, conservatives, and
bigots. Many white workers viewed MLK and black struggles for
equal rights as a threat. Liberals criticized King and other civil
rights leaders for pushing too far, too fast. For instance, fearing
he would lose the political support of Southerners within his
Democratic Party, John F. Kennedy was only a reluctant supporter of the civil rights movement. Like Franklin D. Roosevelt
a generation before, Kennedy had no desire to see thousands
upon thousands of demonstrators on his front lawn demanding
that the federal government take action to end racism. While he
could not stop the March on Washington, Kennedy (and later
Lyndon Johnson) pressured civil rights leaders to tone down their
rhetoric and curtail the radical tendencies within their midst.

Blacks overall regard Martin and certainly Malcolm with
greater reverence and depth of feeling. But, regrettably, they
have not wrestled with the full complexity of the ideas and lives

of these two men who have played such a critical role in the development of the American revolutionary movement. As a result, contemporary African American politicians and public intellectuals have summarily failed to do what Martin and Malcolm (and Jimmy Boggs) did in their lifetimes—namely, move the debates and strategies about black struggle beyond the fight against racism to address the broader concern of how to transform and how to govern the whole of U.S. society. Every American needs a full appreciation of Martin and Malcolm to contribute to making the next American Revolution.

During the 1960s Jimmy and I had paid little attention to the speeches and writings of Dr. Martin Luther King Jr. Like other members of the Detroit black community, made up largely of former Alabamians, we rejoiced at the victories the civil rights movement was winning in the South. For example, I was one of the organizers of the huge June 23, 1963, Freedom Now march down Woodward Avenue in Detroit that was planned by the Detroit Council for Human Rights and led by Dr. King, arm in arm with labor leader Walter Reuther and Detroit Black Power leaders.

However, as activists struggling for Black Power in Detroit, we identified much more with Malcolm X and tended to view King's call for nonviolence and for the beloved community as somewhat naive and sentimental. Neither Jimmy nor I was involved in the fifteen-year campaign that Detroit representative John Conyers Jr. launched in 1968 to declare King's birthday on January 15 a national holiday. I recall holding back because I was concerned that a King holiday would obscure the role of grassroots activists and reinforce the tendency to rely on charismatic leaders. Meanwhile, however, I became increasingly troubled by the way that black militants kept quoting Malcolm's "by all means necessary," ignoring the profound changes that Malcolm was undergoing in the year following his split with the Nation of Islam. Like Martin, like every true revolutionary, Malcolm was a work in progress.

From the moment I first heard Malcolm speak at a huge Nation of Islam rally in the old Olympia Stadium in Detroit, I was captivated by the razor-sharp yet playful language with which he exposed and opposed white society. Later, at smaller meetings, I was fascinated by the way he chided blacks for their "slave mentality," calling them "brainwashed" because they depended so much on whites. They squirmed as he criticized them. But they also laughed and applauded because his criticisms were so right-on and because they knew he was challenging them to look in the mirror and think for themselves, instead of catering to their weaknesses, as most black leaders still do.

From his best-selling autobiography, millions know that while in prison, in his early twenties, Malcolm was transformed from a petty hustler into a black nationalist leader by the ideas of Elijah Muhammad and the Nation of Islam. However, few people know how seriously he began thinking for himself after he discovered in 1963 that Mr. Muhammad had fathered children with his secretaries.

It was during those two years that I had the most direct and indirect contact with Malcolm. In the spring and summer of 1963, Max Stanford of the Revolutionary Action Movement came for long discussions with Jimmy at our home in Detroit while he was deeply engaged in talks with Malcolm in New York. Out of these talks came the new ideas about revolution in Malcolm's speech anticipating his break with the Nation of Islam at the

Grassroots Leadership Conference held in Detroit on November 10, 1963. I was one of the main organizers and Jimmy was the chair of the conference.

The next spring, together with Max Stanford, *Baltimore Afro-American* reporter William Worthy, and Patricia Robinson of Third World Press, Jimmy and I met with Malcolm in a Harlem luncheonette to discuss our proposal that in the light of his break with the Nation of Islam, he come to Detroit to help build the Organization for Black Power. After thinking it over, Malcolm declined because he felt it more important that he make the hajj. His response was that we should go ahead while he served the movement as an "evangelist."

In the fall of 1964, Malcolm's friend Milton Henry and I called him in Egypt to ask him to run for the U.S. Senate on the ticket of the Michigan Freedom Now Party, the "all-black" political party that I served as coordinator. Again he declined, without explaining why.

Later I learned that in this period Malcolm was rethinking the ideas about black nationalism and violence with which most people still identify him. During the hajj he had discovered that revolutionaries come in all colors. He had also begun to recognize the contradictions in "meet violence with violence" politics. As a result, in December 1964, only two months before he was killed, he went to Selma, Alabama, to explore working with Martin Luther King Jr. At this time King was in jail, but Malcolm was able to meet with Coretta.

By this time he had also become painfully aware of the hard theoretical work needed to develop a new body of ideas. In a conversation with Jan Carew in London a few weeks before his assassination, Malcolm explained how he was still growing personally and politically:

I'm a Muslim and a revolutionary, and I'm learning more and more about political theories as the months go by. The only Marxist group in America that offered me a platform was the Socialist Workers party. I respect them and they respect me. The Communists have nixed me, gone out of the way to attack me . . . that is, with the exception of the Cuban Communists. If a mixture of nationalism and Marxism makes the Cubans fight the way they do and makes the Vietnamese stand up so resolutely to the might of America and its European and other lapdogs, then there must be something to it. But my Organization of African American Unity is based in Harlem and we've got to learn to creep before we walk, and walk before we run. . . . But the chances are that they will get me the way they got Lumumba before he reached the running stage.[1]

This kind of introspection, questioning, and transformation, which were so characteristic of Malcolm, has unfortunately been ignored by too many black nationalists and Black Power militants. Every February, as another anniversary of his death passes, I have wondered if our world would be different today had Malcolm lived into his fifties and sixties.

Meanwhile, as violence in Detroit and other cities escalated in the wake of the urban rebellions, I also began to wonder: Might events have taken a different path if we had found a way to infuse our struggle for Black Power with King's philosophy of nonviolence? Is it possible that our relationships with one another today, not only inter- but intraracially, would be more harmonious if we had discovered how to blend Malcolm's militancy with King's vision of the beloved community? Could such a synthesis have a revolutionary power beyond our wildest dreams? Is such a revolutionary power available to us today?

My interest in King was especially piqued by the little pamphlet *A Way of Faith, a Time for Courage* published in 1984 by the Seattle chapter of the National Organization for an American

Revolution. In this pamphlet our old friends Vincent and Rose-mary Harding, who had worked closely with MLK in the 1960s, explain that "Martin wasn't assassinated for simply wanting black and white children to hold hands, but because he said that there must be fundamental changes in this country and that black people must take the lead in bringing them. . . . Put simply, these problems are Racism, Materialism, Militarism, and Anti-Communism."[2]

In 1983 Reagan signed into law the decision to observe King's birthday as a national holiday, and scholars started reevaluating his work and life.[3]

In 1992, at the opening ceremony of Detroit Summer, I had noted the similarity between our vision and King's projections for direct youth action "in our dying cities."

In the spring of 1998, when I was asked what I thought about the Black Radical Congress, I replied that to create a new move-ment, we must first understand the old. For movement activists in our period, this means grappling with the significance of the Black Panther Party, Malcolm X, and King.[4]

As a result of all these developments, I began studying King's life and work from the perspective of our work in Detroit. To my delight I discovered that Hegel had been King's favorite philosopher. This reminded me of the influence that Hegel has had on my own life ever since I read his *Phenomenology* in my early twenties and learned that the process of constantly over-coming contradictions, or what Hegel called "the suffering, the patience, and the labour of the negative," is the key to the con-tinuing evolution of humanity.[5]

I discovered that King, particularly during the last three years of his life, had viewed the American preoccupation with rapid economic advancement as the source of our deepening crises both at home and in our relationships with the rest of the world.

I also discovered how much King had learned from Gandhi's critique of Western civilization. We are constantly being reminded, and rightly so, that Gandhi's successful use of nonviolent civil disobedience in the struggle for independence from Britain convinced King of the power that Truth exercises when united with practical actions. King had drawn mainly on Gandhi's ideas of nonviolence during his civil rights years. After 1966 he still emphasized nonviolence, but he began to draw more on Gandhi's profound critiques of Western civilization.

In 1888, when Gandhi was the age of today's average American college student, his family wanted him to succeed in the system. So they sent him to London to study law. Eager to justify the sacrifices his family was making, Gandhi tried to transform himself into an English gentleman. He signed up for a dancing class, bought himself a silk hat, and spent ten minutes every day before a huge mirror watching himself arrange his tie and parting his hair in the correct fashion. In a passage from his autobiography, amazingly similar to the one in which Malcolm X describes pouring lye on his kinky hair to make it as straight as any white man's, Gandhi writes, "My hair was by no means soft, and every day it meant a regular struggle with the brush to keep it in position."[6]

However, after returning to India with his law degree and finding it difficult to make a living, Gandhi decided to try his luck in South Africa, where there was a sizable community of Indian workers imported to do the menial work deemed below the dignity of Europeans. As he experienced racist violence against himself and witnessed it against Indian workers and blacks, he began to identify with the most oppressed and conquered his feelings of inadequacy and his fear of the system. He recognized the moral bankruptcy of those in power and separated himself from their values.

In this process, which continued after he returned to India, Gandhi created a new form of struggle based not on physical violence but on the spiritual power of Truth and Love (which he called *satyagraha*) and developed personal habits, such as celibacy and vegetarianism, that enabled him to experience the freedom and power that come from self-discipline. He also arrived at amazingly prescient critiques of Western civilization and Western strategies for revolutionary struggle.

The main reason why Western civilization lacks Spirituality, or an awareness of our interconnectedness with one another and the universe, according to Gandhi, is that it has given priority to economic and technological development over human and community development. Advanced technology has made it possible for people to perform miracles, but it has impoverished us spiritually because it has made us feel that outside forces determine who and what we are. Traditional societies lacked our material comforts and conveniences, but individuals had more Soul, or a belief in the individual's power to make moral choices, because these societies valued the community relationships that they depended on for survival.

Because modern societies, capitalist or communist, are committed to unlimited growth, Gandhi anticipated that they would eventually become so gigantic and complex that human beings would be reduced to masses, dependent on experts, serving machines instead of being served by them. Moreover, the abundance created by pursuing unlimited economic growth would make it almost impossible for people to distinguish between Needs and Wants, so that they would end up being enslaved by the temptations of material wealth and luxuries, a form of bondage he considered even more cruel than physical enslavement.

For similar reasons, Gandhi rejected Western strategies for revolutionary struggle that depend on constantly agitating the masses and increasing their anger, militancy, and rebellion. Struggles of this kind, he said, could only end up with political leaders who are preoccupied with prestige and power and with states dominating rather than serving society. The struggle for independence from Britain, he insisted, should not be mainly a struggle for state power. It should revolve around going to people at the grassroots, helping them to transform their inner and outer lives, and encouraging them to think for themselves in order to create self-reliant local communities. Such communities should be based on two pillars: Work that preserves rather than destroys skills while fostering cooperation rather than competition and Education whose goal is the building of community rather than increasing the status and earning power of the individual. Stressing the importance of human relations beyond the nation-state, Gandhi began projecting a new concept of global citizenship— one that especially appealed to Martin Luther King Jr.

As King's life and ideas became more meaningful to me, I began speaking about him at MLK holiday celebrations and on other occasions. For example, at the University of Michigan 2003 MLK Symposium, my speech was titled "We Must Be the Change." At Union Theological Seminary in September 2006, I spoke on "Catching Up with Martin." At Eastern Michigan University in January 2007, I emphasized the need to "Recapture MLK's Radical Revolutionary Spirit/Create Cities and Communities of Hope." At the Brecht Forum in May 2007, my speech was titled "Let's Talk about Malcolm and Martin." The more I talked about King and engaged in conversations with the people

I encountered at these gatherings, the more I felt the need for each of us to grow our own souls to overcome the new and more challenging contradictions of constantly changing realities.

The Montgomery Bus Boycott (1955–56), I realized, was the first struggle by an oppressed people in Western society based on the concept of two-sided transformation, both of ourselves and of our institutions. Inspired by the twenty-six-year-old King, a people who had been treated as less than human had struggled for more than a year against their dehumanization, not as angry protesters or as workers in the plant, but as members of the Montgomery community, new men and women representing a more human society in evolution. They created their own system of transportation—one that transformed themselves and increased the good rather than the evil in the world. They used methods that exercised their spiritual power, always bearing in mind that their goal was not only desegregating buses but also building the beloved community. In this way, they inspired the human identity, antiwar, and ecological movements that during the last decade of the twentieth century were giving birth to a new civil society in the United States.

The more I studied King's life and ideas, especially in the last three years before his assassination, the more I also recognized the similarity between our struggles in Detroit after the 1967 rebellion and King's after the 1965 Watts uprising. On August 6, 1965, nearly a decade after the Montgomery Bus Boycott, King was among the black and white leaders who joined President Johnson in celebrating the signing of the Voting Rights Act, the result of the march from Selma to Montgomery. Less than a week later, on August 11, black youth in Watts, California, protesting the police arrest of a speeding driver, exploded in an uprising in which thirty-four people died and thousands were arrested.

When King flew to Watts on August 15, he discovered to his surprise that few black youth in Watts had even heard of him or his strategy of nonviolence and that, despite the loss of lives, they were claiming victory because their violence had forced the authorities to acknowledge their existence.

The Watts uprising forced King to recognize how little attention he himself had paid to black youth in the cities. So in early 1966 he rented an apartment in the Chicago ghetto and was able to get a sense of how the anger that exploded in Watts was rooted in the powerlessness and uselessness that is the daily experience of black youth made expendable by technology.

He wrote up his findings in *Where Do We Go from Here: Community or Chaos?* Published in early 1967, it begins with King's recognition that with Selma and the Voting Rights Act we had come to the end of the protest phase of the civil rights revolution and entered into a new phase that requires structural changes in the system to eliminate poverty and unemployment and close the gap between rich and poor in this country and around the world.

Bringing about these changes, King explains, will require more than demands for Black Power, which although emotionally gratifying, are often more an expression of disappointment and despair than of the hope and vision necessary to mobilize people in struggle. Our challenge, King said, is to organize the strength and compelling power of poor people, white as well as black, as workers, consumers, and voters, to make demands on the government for sweeping measures, such as a guaranteed annual income for everyone. We need to turn "the ghettos into a vast school" to make "every street corner into a forum" and "every houseworker and every laborer a demonstrator, a voter, a canvasser and a student."[7]

However, to be successful in this organizing effort, we have to go beyond usual politics and "undergo a mental and spiritual re-evaluation." We need to recognize, as King did, that "the richer we have become materially, the poorer we have become morally and spiritually," so that we can begin working systematically "to bridge the huge gulf between our scientific progress and our moral progress." What this ultimately means is that we must undergo "a revolution of values." Warning that material growth had been made an end in itself and that our scientific power had outrun our spiritual power, King rejected the dictatorship of Hi-Tech, which he said diminishes people because it eliminates the sense of participation. "Enlarged material powers," he warned repeatedly, "spell enlarged peril if there is no proportionate growth of the soul." We have "guided missiles and misguided men." We must begin the shift from what King called a "thing"-oriented society to a "person"-oriented society. "When machines and computers, profit motives and property rights are considered more important than people," he declared, "the giant triplets of racism, materialism and militarism are incapable of being conquered."[8]

This revolution of values must take us beyond traditional capitalism and communism. Capitalism, he said, "encourages a cutthroat competition and selfish ambition that inspire men to be more I-centered than thou-centered." Communism, as it had been instituted by parties in state power, had reduced men to "a cog in the wheel of the state." "Each represents a partial truth," concluded King. "Communism fails to see the truth in individualism. Capitalism fails to realize that life is social."[9]

Charting a new direction for the movement, King called for rethinking the meaning of work. He pushed us to move beyond the notion of labor principally as an exchange value, an invention of free-market capitalism that has alienated human beings from each other and from Nature while diminishing our capacities for self-reliance. Quoting the nineteenth-century political economist Henry George, King advocated "work which improves the conditions of mankind"—the kind of "work which extends knowledge and increases power and enriches literature and elevates thought." This kind of work "is not done to secure a living," King continued. "It is not the work of slaves, driven to their task either by the lash of a master or by animal necessities. It is the work of men who perform it for their own sake and not that they may get more to eat or drink or wear or display. In a state of society where want is abolished, work of this sort could be enormously increased." King concluded by outlining a need for "new forms of work that enhance the social good . . . to be devised for those for whom traditional jobs are not available"—those such as the structurally unemployed, ex-cons, and youth lashing out in urban rebellion.[10]

In Chicago, King also discovered the futility of trying to involve these dispossessed young people in the kinds of non-violent mass marches that had worked in the South. And they gave him a lot to think about when they demanded to know why they should be nonviolent in Chicago when the U.S. government was employing such massive violence against poor peasants in Vietnam.

Thus, King's "A Time to Break Silence," his soul-stirring antiwar speech at Riverside Church on April 4, 1967, was the result of his wrestling not only with the Vietnam War but also with the questions raised by these young people in what he called "our dying cities."

"The war in Vietnam," he recognized, "is but a symptom of a far deeper malady within the American spirit. We are on the wrong side of a world revolution because we refuse to give up the privileges and the pleasures that come from the immense profits of overseas investment.

"We have come to value things more than people. Our technological development has outrun our spiritual development. We have lost our sense of community, of interconnection and participation."[11]

To get on the right side of that revolution, we as a nation must undergo a radical revolution of values, King emphasized again.

Then comes a passage in which by simply replacing the word "communism" with "terrorism," King could be talking to us today. "This kind of positive revolution of values is our best defense against communism. War is not the answer. Communism will never be defeated by the use of atomic bombs or nuclear weapons.... We must not engage in a negative anti-communism, but rather in a positive thrust for democracy, realizing that our greatest defense against communism is to take offensive action in behalf of justice. We must with positive action seek to remove those conditions of poverty, insecurity and injustice which are the fertile soil in which the seed of communism grows and develops."[12]

If over the past forty years we had heeded these words, if instead of pursuing the cold war against communism we had created a movement to reorder our priorities, if we had started to live more simply so that others could simply live, terrorism would not have had such a fertile soil in which to grow.

By drawing on the transformational ideas of Hegel, Gandhi, and Jesus Christ, all of which had become more meaningful to him since the Montgomery Bus Boycott, King began to develop a profoundly cultural and political concept of the next American Revolution. Drawing from Gandhi's critique of Western culture and from Hegel's dialectical thought, he developed a powerful vision of how a racist, militaristic, and materialist world—tormented by violence and alienation—could be transformed through the redemptive human capacity for Love.

King began to connect the despair and violence in the urban ghettos with the alienation that young people experience. The sixties generation, he said, was "engaged in a cold war" with their elders, but their rebellion did not emanate from "the familiar and normal hostility of the young groping for independence." The youth exhibited "a new quality of bitter antagonism and confused anger," which suggested to King that basic values were under contestation. He urged us to recognize the source of this alienation: "Nothing in our glittering society can raise man to new heights, because material growth has been made an end in itself, and in the absence of moral purpose, man himself becomes smaller as the works of man become bigger."[13]

With a heightened sense of economic insecurity giving rise to new and dangerous expressions of demagoguery in 2010, King's words sound even more prophetic. The way to overcome this alienation, he said, is by changing our priorities. Instead of pursuing economic productivity, we need to expand our uniquely human powers, especially our capacity for Love. Most people think of Love only in terms of affection, between lovers *(eros)* or friends *(philia)*. However, King's experiences as a black man in racist America had taught him that love of power goes hand in hand with dominating and destroying community. So he developed a concept of Love (he called it "Agape"), which is based on the willingness to go to any lengths to restore or create community. Practicing this concept of Love empowers the oppressed to overcome Fear and the oppressors to transcend Hate.

This Love, King insisted, is not some sentimental weakness but somehow the key to ultimate reality. We can learn its practical meaning from the young people who joined the civil rights movement, putting "middle-class values" of wealth and careers in second place, taking off their "Brooks Brother attire" and putting on "overalls to work in the isolated rural South" because they felt the need for more direct ways of learning that would strengthen both society and themselves. What we need now in "our dying cities," he said, are ways to provide young people with similar opportunities to engage in "direct self-transforming and structure-transforming action."[14]

In practice, taking this statement of King's seriously requires a radical change or paradigm shift in our approach to organizing and our definition of citizenship, which is the practice of politics. Instead of pursuing rapid economic development and hoping that it will eventually create community, we need to do the opposite—begin with the needs of the community and create loving relationships with one another and with the Earth.

As Jimmy Boggs used to remind us, revolutions are made out of love for people and for place. He often talked about loving America enough to change it. "I love this country," he used to say, "not only because my ancestors' blood is in the soil but because of what I believe it can become." Shea Howell, Oakland University rhetoric professor and former director of Detroit Summer, has helped hundreds of students and community organizers appreciate what Jimmy meant: Love isn't just something you feel. It's something you do every day when you go out and pick up the papers and bottles scattered the night before on the corner, when you stop and talk to a neighbor, when you argue passionately for what you believe with whoever will listen, when you call a friend to see how they're doing, when you write a letter to the newspaper, when you give a speech and give 'em hell, when you never stop believing that we can all be more than we are. In other words, Love isn't about what we did yesterday; it's about what we do today and tomorrow and the day after.

Taking King seriously also requires a paradigm shift in how we address the three main questions of philosophy: What does it mean to be a human being? How do we know? How shall we live? It means rejecting scientific rationalism (based on the Cartesian body-mind dichotomy), which recognizes as real only that which can be measured and therefore excludes the knowledge that comes from the heart or from relationships between people. It means that we must be willing to see with our hearts and not only with our eyes.

King was assassinated before he could begin to develop strategies and praxis to implement this revolutionary/evolutionary perspective for our young people, our cities, and our country. After his death many of his closest associates were too overwhelmed or too busy taking advantage of the new opportunities for advancement within the system to keep his vision and his practice alive.

We will never know how King would have developed had he lived to see the twenty-first century. What we do know is that in the forty years since his assassination, our communities have been turned into wastelands by the Hi-Tech juggernaut and the export of, first, factory and, now, computer jobs overseas so that global corporations can make more of a profit with cheaper labor. We have witnessed and shared the suffering of countless numbers of young people in our inner cities, who in their struggle to survive have resorted to hustling and ended up in prisons. We have watched our young people shooting baskets 24/7, with dreams of making it in the NBA. We don't know whether to weep or rejoice as we watch others, such as the late Tupac Shakur, struggling to make it in the hip-hop world.

Like King after the Watts uprising of 1965, we have wondered what we should say to the 30 to 50 percent of inner-city youth who reject the pleas and promises of the Establishment and their parents to stay in schools and get their diplomas so that they can get a good job, make a lot of money, and move out of our disintegrating communities. And it is not only inner-city youth. Suburban schools are riddled with substance abuse and haunted by fears of another Columbine. On campuses, young people with bachelor's degrees, unable to find meaningful work and unwilling to accept work without meaning, linger on to become professional students.

Since the terrorist attack of 9/11, we have also wondered what kind of transformation of ourselves and our institutions we need to preserve the best in our history and provide the blessings of liberty and security for ourselves and our posterity. Studies have revealed that many Americans, faced with mortality on such an instant and colossal scale, began reassessing their priorities and wondering how to make their lives more meaningful. As a result, growing numbers began to recognize that spiritual values such as compassion, generosity, and community are more important than material consumption.

And as George W. Bush's ceaseless pursuit of war, exploitation of popular fears, and attack on civil liberties alienated a majority of both the world's population and the American people, it became increasingly clear that the best way to ensure our safety and peace of mind is not by warring on the "axis of evil" but by making a radical revolution in our own values. In the days ahead, everyone who loves this country enough to change it will have many opportunities both to reflect on and to practice the radical revolution in values that King projected and to foster a concept of global citizenship in which the life of an Afghani, Iraqi, Iranian, North Korean, or Palestinian is considered as precious as that of an American. We need to discuss these ideas with our coworkers, neighbors, families, church members, and others because together we can create the new language that describes the kind of new human beings and the kind of country we want to become.

Our study of King's life and works can teach us invaluable lessons for building a movement in this moment of danger and opportunity:

- King was very clear that suffering and oppression are not enough to create a movement. African Americans began the Montgomery Bus Boycott because they had *"replaced self-pity with self-respect and self-depreciation with dignity."* [15] In other words, a movement begins when the oppressed begin seeing themselves not just as victims but as new men and women—pioneers in creating new, more human relations and thus advancing the evolution of the human race.

- Movement builders are also very conscious of the need to go beyond slogans and to create programs of struggle that transform and empower participants. The Montgomery Bus Boycott, for example, created an alternative self-reliant transportation system. When Jimmy and I helped launch Detroit Summer in 1992 to promote youth leadership and new visions for the city, we were inspired by King's last speeches addressing the alienation of urban youth—to give young people in "our dying cities" opportunities to engage in "self-transforming and structure-transforming" direct action.

· Confident of their own humanity, movement builders are able to recognize the humanity in others, including their opponents, and therefore the potential within them for redemption. So they hate unjust deeds but are careful not to hate the doers of these deeds. And they choose to struggle nonviolently because they know that nonviolent struggles can become swords that heal, enabling both sides to grow to humanity's full stature and restoring community, while violent struggles increase the hate, fear, and bitterness in the world.

· At the heart of movement building is the concept of two-sided transformation, both of ourselves and of our institutions. Even though justice is on our side, we recognize that we are also products of this society. That is why we make sure that the methods we use in our struggles are transforming ourselves as well as our opponents into *more human* human beings.

· Thinking dialectically is also pivotal to movement building because it prepares us for the contradictions that inevitably develop in the course of a struggle. A struggle that starts with the needs of a particular ethnic or social group only becomes a movement if it creates Hope and the vision of a new society for everyone. But great hopes can also lead to great disappointments. Thus, the black rebellions and the call for Black Power that exploded in northern cities after 1965 expressed the frustration and desperation of urban black youth whose needs were not being met by the civil rights movement.

In the end, I hope that I have helped in some small way to stimulate a deeper conversation about Malcolm and Martin. Talking about these two American revolutionaries is a key means by which we can revisit the great unanswered questions from the late sixties, when a macho concept of power, biological thinking (in which race and color dictate loyalty), electoral politics, and the pursuit of upward mobility into the burning house of U.S. capitalism took over from the politics of the two-sided transformation of ourselves and our institutions that both Malcolm and Martin were creating at the grassroots level. This revisiting is an important part of what we are doing with our Detroit–City of Hope campaign, sparked by commemorations of the fortieth anniversaries of the 1967 Detroit Rebellion and King's "A Time to Break Silence" speech.

All around me, I am filled with a sense of Hope as I see growing numbers of Detroiters carrying on the legacy of Malcolm and Martin by confronting new contradictions through their words and deeds.

For instance, Yusef Shakur's journey, like Malcolm's, has been one of Transformation and Resurrection. His self-published book *The Window 2 My Soul: My Transformation from a Zone 8 Thug to a Father & Freedom Fighter* is the twenty-first-century story of a new generation of "Outsiders" born since the 1960s.[16]

Yusef has coined new words like "shit-uation" and "overstand" to open our eyes to the world of single mothers and absent fathers into which he was born. His mother gave birth to him when she was only fifteen years old. He was named Joseph Lee Ruffin after his mother's father and nicknamed JoJo. His own father, Richard Lee Carter—only seventeen years old—had left for the navy. To provide food, clothing, and shelter for him and his sister (by another man), JoJo's mother sold her body to men who used her as a punching bag. She became an alcoholic but never stopped caring for her son.

Growing up on the mean streets of Detroit, where factory jobs had disappeared and crack was king, JoJo's education came from the thugs and predators in Zone 8 (Detroit zip code 48208). So it was natural for him to believe that preying on one another and meeting violence with violence was the way to survive. He was able to "rebuild himself from the inside out" only after he was incarcerated (for a crime he did not but could have committed) and was schooled in prison by his father, who had been incarcerated when JoJo was ten years old and had overcome self-hate by becoming a Muslim.

Window 2 My Soul is the story of an Outsider rebuilding, redefining, respiriting himself. Whether you grew up in a hood, a suburb, or a gated community, it will help you discover how you can begin to free yourself and our country from the "dog-eat-dog," hyperindividualistic, hypermaterialistic, Darwinian, survivalist, violent, capitalist culture, which is destroying our humanity and all life on our planet.

Malcolm, also a thoughtful reader, was murdered before he was forty, leaving it to us to keep transforming our selves, as he was doing to the very end. Yusef is thirty-seven, still with us, still evolving. As a community activist, he has organized programs to help incarcerated men and their loved ones keep their lives and families in order. As a Head Start teacher, he has helped to nourish small children growing up in Detroit. Today, Yusef continues to inspire others because he walks the talk. He is developing community-minded arts and entrepreneurship while spreading his message through public forums, outreaching to youth, and launching a community garden.

Meanwhile, I have watched the urgency of the Black Power movement come together with King's vision of revolutionary nonviolence through the work of Ron Scott. Ron helped organize the Black Panther Party chapter in Detroit, where the local branch emphasized the creation of community-building survival programs over militant posturing.

Ron has since become a leading figure in the Coalition against Police Brutality, which is devoted to the creation of Peace Zones for Life. After repeatedly mobilizing demonstrations and filing lawsuits against the authorities, the organization launched this project after finding that many instances of police violence occurred in response to calls regarding domestic conflicts. Thus, to get at the root cause of police abuse, the organization seeks to reduce and eliminate the need for citizens to call the police in the first place. It promotes "community-based conflict resolution and mediation initiatives," using "methods that will allow the citizens options to submit their grievances for resolution by their neighbors or persons whom they trust; thereby, remaining outside the police/criminal justice system and eliminating conflict within our communities."[17]

Moreover, the organization seeks to involve neighborhood youth themselves, many of whom had once been sucked into gangs or drug dealing, in conflict resolution practices and community-oriented, small-business development. Above all, Peace Zones for Life is a grassroots initiative driven by people who are taking responsibility for the social, economic, and physical health of their community. It does not assume that inner-city residents themselves are solely responsible for the deterioration of neighborhoods ravaged by decades of race, class, and gender oppression, but it does insist that they are necessary change agents to remedy our crisis situation.

The idea of Peace Zones is a transformative one that builds on the concept of restorative justice. In response to the cancerous growth of the prison industry and the now widely recognized problem of overcrowded prisons siphoning away scarce public resources, the restorative justice movement offers methods to heal both ex-offenders and their communities. Our present criminal justice system is based on the concept of punitive or retributive justice. Punitive justice views antisocial behavior as an offense against the state, which therefore has the right and responsibility to punish offenders and which does so primarily by isolating them. But now that prisons clearly serve as warehouses for the millions whom capitalism has made expendable, now that our families and communities are being devastated by the incarceration (often for nonviolent offenses) of millions of brothers, sisters, mothers, and fathers, our survival depends on our making a paradigm shift in our whole approach to justice. We need to take it upon ourselves to practice a concept of justice that will empower offenders and the community to work together to build a healthy community.

From these critical examples, you can get a glimpse of how in Detroit we are not just celebrating history. We are learning from the legacy of Malcolm and Martin and writing a new chapter of human history.

CHAPTER FOUR

Detroit, Place and
Space to Begin Anew

Detroit is a city of Hope rather than a city of Despair. The thousands of vacant lots and abandoned houses provide not only the space to begin anew but also the incentive to create innovative ways of making our living—ways that nurture our productive, cooperative, and caring selves.

The media and pundits keep repeating that today's economic meltdown is the worst financial crisis since the Great Depression. But in the 1930s the United States was an overproducing industrial giant, not today's casino economy. In the past few decades, once-productive Americans have been transformed into consumers, using more and more of the resources of the Earth to foster ways of living that are unsustainable and unsatisfying. This way of life has created suburbs that destroy farmland, wetlands, and the natural world, as well as pollute the environment. The new economy also requires a huge military apparatus to secure global resources and to consume materials for itself, at the same time providing enormous riches for arms merchants and for our otherwise failing auto, aircraft, and ship manufacturers.

Instead of trying to resurrect or reform a system whose endless pursuit of economic growth has created a nation of material abundance and spiritual poverty—and instead of hoping for a new FDR to save capitalism with New Deal–like programs—we need to build a new kind of economy from the ground up.

That is what I have learned from fifty-five years of living and struggling in Detroit, the city that was once the national and international symbol of the miracle of industrialization and is now the national and international symbol of the devastation of deindustrialization. That is why so many people, especially young people, have their eyes on Detroit today.

THE END OF THE INDUSTRIAL AGE

I came to Detroit in the early 1950s because as a Marxist I wanted to be part of a revolution in which the workers in the auto factories would take the struggles of the 1930s to a higher level by struggling for workers' control of production in the plant. My main difference with traditional Marxists was my belief that blacks, women, and young people, and not only workers, would play pivotal roles in this revolution.

Living with Jimmy Boggs, who was active both in the Chrysler Jefferson plant and in the community, it was not long before I realized that my ideas had come mostly out of books and that my expectations had little or no relationship to the reality that was rapidly changing all around me.

The workforce in the factories, instead of expanding and becoming more centralized, was being decimated by automation and decentralized by plant relocations. At the same time, Detroit itself was becoming predominantly black as middle-class and working-class whites fled to the suburbs, aided and abetted by the government providing Federal Housing Administration mortgages and spending billions of tax dollars on freeway construction to help the auto industry expand. As a result, the predominantly white police force began to act like an occupation army, and the white city government began to resemble a colonial administration, thus setting the stage for the Black Power movement, which we began organizing in Detroit in the early 1960s.

As we struggled for black political power in Detroit in the 1960s, we were not thinking about how we would reorganize the economy. Our main concern was that despite the growing black population, those governing the city and the schools remained almost exclusively white. When whites asked us how Black Power would differ from white power, our reply was usually a superficial "It couldn't be any worse."

Then on July 20, 1967, while Jimmy and I were on vacation in California, Detroit cops raided a blind pig on Twelfth Street, now Rosa Parks Boulevard, and all hell broke loose. Thousands of Detroiters, predominantly young people, poured into the streets and began looting stores and torching large sections of the city. Before it was over, the National Guard and federal troops had been called in, over twenty-five hundred buildings had been looted and burned, and forty-three people had been killed. The media called it a "riot," but Detroiters called it a "rebellion" because it was an understandable response by young people to the brutality and racism of a mostly white police force (or occupation army) and also to their growing sense that they were being made expendable by Hi-Tech.[1]

More than any picketing or marching or organizing that we did, it was the spontaneous explosion of young Detroiters that ensured the election of Detroit's first black mayor because it told the Establishment that white political power could no longer maintain law and order in the city.

In 1973 Coleman A. Young was elected Detroit's first black mayor. A former autoworker and one of the Tuskegee Airmen, Coleman was a charismatic and forceful militant, who had been closely associated with the left wing of the labor movement. But it soon became clear that despite his militancy and progressive views, he lacked the historical imagination to create the new vision that would light a path for Detroiters through the thickets of the new stage of multinational capitalism.

Coleman acted decisively to reverse the racism imbedded within the fire and police departments and in city administration, applying affirmative action to create racial equity in the hiring and appointment of public employees. But even though he was one of this country's brightest and most skillful politicians (some people say that if he had not been black, he would have been elected president), he was helpless in the face of the deindustrialization and outsourcing that were gaining momentum in the 1970s. Because he had failed to think seriously about the profound changes taking place in the economy, he had no idea how to deal with the new information technology and the massive export of jobs overseas that was making it impossible for young people to find meaningful paid work in the city.

All Coleman could do was react, and he was ultimately driven to desperate measures to try to replace the jobs that were gone for good. For example, in 1980–81, with the support of the United Auto Workers, he made a disastrous decision to bulldoze the Poletown community—an integrated section of the city adjacent to the working-class and historically Polish town of Hamtramck. With the mayor leading the way, the Poletown project destroyed nearly twelve hundred buildings and displaced more than one hundred businesses and thirteen hundred households. Over the staunch and dramatic protests of residents, an entire community was leveled to provide General Motors with the space to build a plant that it promised would provide six thousand jobs. In fact, it barely delivered half that amount at its peak. Meanwhile, GM issued a series of layoffs to workers at its Fisher Body and Cadillac plants that far outweighed the significance of the new jobs created.[2] The whole Poletown fiasco was a very dramatic example of destroying a community in a futile effort to bring back the past.

As jobs continued to disappear, the city experienced the next casualty of deindustrialization. Because kids with a high school degree or less could no longer get a factory job that paid enough to get married and raise a family, many were seduced by the seemingly easy riches the drug trade offered when crack came to Detroit in 1985. These despairing and desperate youth began to ask, "Why stay in school with the idea that one day you'll get a job making a lot of money when you can make a lot of money now rolling?" By the thousands they began dropping out of high school, creating a drug economy that brought forth a huge spurt in violence and homicides. In 1986 alone, 43 children were killed and 365 wounded.

Faced with this deteriorating situation, Coleman became even more desperate. In 1988 he proposed the development of Las Vegas–style casinos to provide the jobs that the auto industry no longer provided. Gaming was an "industry," he insisted, that would create fifty thousand jobs. By contrast, Jimmy Boggs had the audacity to claim that "a job ain't the answer." While most people saw (and still see) jobs as the answer to racism, poverty, and inequality, we needed to understand that jobs no longer play the role they did in periods of scarcity. We needed to measure the worth of a human being in very different ways.

To defeat Coleman's casino gambling initiative, Jimmy and I helped to build a new formation called Detroiters Uniting. We described ourselves as a coalition of community groups—blue collar, white collar, and cultural workers; clergy members; political leaders; and professionals—who together embodied the rich ethnic and social diversity of our city. The principal concern of Detroiters Uniting was with "how our city has been disintegrating socially, economically, politically, morally and ethically."[3] In the citywide referendum we were able to defeat the mayor's casino proposal.

But during the struggle Coleman called us a bunch of naysayers and demanded to know "What is your alternative?"

It was a very good question, helping, indeed forcing, us to recognize that we were at one of the great turning points in history. Detroit's deindustrialization, devastation, and depopulation had turned the city into a wasteland, but it had also created the space and place where there was not only the necessity but also the possibility of creating a city based not on expanding production but on new values of sustainability and community. Instead of investing our hopes in GM, Ford, and Chrysler and becoming increasingly alienated from each other and the Earth, we needed to invest in, work with, and rely on each other. Through no fault of our own, we had been granted an opportunity to begin a new chapter in the evolution of the human race, a chapter that global warming and corporate globalization had made increasingly necessary. In its dying, Detroit could also be the birthplace of a new kind of city.

"We are convinced," Detroiters Uniting declared, "that we cannot depend upon one industry or one large corporation to

provide us with jobs. It is now up to us—the citizens of Detroit—
to put our hearts, our imaginations, our minds, and our hands
together to create a vision and project concrete programs for
developing the kinds of local enterprises that will provide meaningful jobs and income for all citizens."[4]

PLANTING SEEDS OF HOPE

During the 1960s Jimmy Boggs had anticipated some of the economic challenges that black political power would face. "The
ability of capitalists today to produce in abundance," he wrote
in "Black Power: A Scientific Concept Whose Time Has Come,"
"has already brought the United States technologically to
the threshold of a society where each can have according
to his needs." Therefore, he concluded, "black political power
will have to decide on the kind of economy and the aims and
direction of the economy for the people."[5] Watching the city's
first African American mayor pursue job creation through the
physical destruction of a community and hasten its spiritual
destruction through gambling—methods that were not only
manifestly parasitic and antihuman but ultimately futile—
Jimmy began envisioning a Detroit founded on different principles. In a 1985 speech, he had said that we needed to go where we
have never gone before and focus on "creating communities."
During the 1988 debate on casino gambling, he projected a
vision of a new kind of city whose foundation would be citizens living in communities who take responsibility for decisions
about their city instead of leaving these to politicians or to the
marketplace and who create small enterprises that emphasize
the preservation of skills and produce goods and services for
the local community.

As Detroiters, we were very conscious of our city as a movement city. Out of the ashes of industrialization we decided to seize the opportunity to create a twenty-first-century city, a city both rural and urban, which attracts people from all over the world because it understands the fundamental need of human beings at this stage in our evolution to relate more responsibly to one another and to the Earth.

In pursuit of this vision, we organized a People's Festival of community organizations in November 1991, describing it as "a Multi-Generational, Multi-Cultural celebration of Detroiters, putting our hearts, minds, hands and imaginations together to redefine and re-create a city of Community, Compassion, Cooperation, Participation and Enterprise in harmony with the Earth."[6] A few months later, to engage young people in the movement to create this new kind of city, we founded Detroit Summer and described it as a multicultural, intergenerational youth program/movement to rebuild, redefine, and respirit Detroit from the ground up.

Through Detroit Summer, urban youth of a lost post-1960s generation, whom many adults had come to shun, fear, and ultimately blame for so many ills, became a part of the solution to Detroit's problems. Recalling how the Freedom Schools of Mississippi Freedom Summer had engaged children in the civil rights movement, we asked Detroiters to just imagine how much safer and livelier our neighborhoods would be almost overnight if we reorganized education along the lines of Detroit Summer; if instead of trying to keep our children isolated in classrooms for twelve years and more, we engaged them in community-building activities with the same audacity with which the civil rights movement engaged them in desegregation activities forty years ago: planting community gardens, recycling waste, organizing neighborhood arts and health festivals, rehabbing houses, and painting public murals.

By giving our children and young people a better reason to learn than just the individualistic one of getting a job or making more money, by encouraging them to make a difference in their neighborhoods, we would get their cognitive juices flowing. Learning would come from practice, which has always been the best way to learn. In Detroit Summer we combined physical forms of work with workshops and intergenerational dialogues on how to rebuild Detroit, thus further expanding the minds and imaginations of the young, old, and in-between. Instead of coercing young people to conform to the factory model of education, the time had come, we said, to see their rebellion as a cry for another kind of education that values them as human beings and gives them opportunities to exercise their Soul Power.

Detroit Summer began in June 1992 and has been an ongoing and developing program for more than fifteen years. Since 2005 it has been organized by a multiracial collective of twenty-something young people, many of whom have been a part of our past summer programs. With this younger generation now at the helm of leadership of the Detroit Summer Collective, the organization continues to tap the creative energies of urban youth. Marshaling their interest and skills in hip-hop and slam poetry, it advances a critical dialogue about burning social issues by empowering youth to express themselves through alternative forms of media.

Some skeptics question whether a program such as Detroit Summer can make much of a difference, given the magnitude of the city's problems. They doubt that a program, which at its height involved sixty youth organizers, could have an appreciable effect in stemming the crises of school dropouts, violence, and incarceration that are stealing lives by the thousands. They ask how tending to a handful of gardens, painting one or two murals a year, and fixing up a house or vacant lot here and there can address the blight that has taken over much of the urban landscape. And they lament that small dialogues—between youth and elders, between neighbors, between people of different backgrounds, and between activists from various cultural and political traditions—cannot match the force of large demonstrations involving tens of thousands.

What they don't understand is that our goal in creating Detroit Summer was to create a new *kind* of organization. We never intended for it to be a traditional left-wing organization agitating masses of youth to protest and demonstrate. Nor did we intend that it become a large nonprofit corporation of the sort that raises millions of dollars from government, corporations, and foundations to provide employment and services to large populations.

Both of these forms of organizing can be readily found in Detroit and all major cities in the United States, but the system continues to function because neither carries the potential to transform society. By contrast, our hope was that Detroit Summer would bring about a new vision and model of community activism—one that was particularly responsive to the new challenges posed by the conditions of life and struggle in the postindustrial city. We did not feel this could be accomplished if control of our activities was ceded to the dictates of government or the private sector, even though this meant that we would be working on a small scale. However, by working on this scale, we could pay much closer and greater attention to the relationships we were building among ourselves and with communities in Detroit and beyond.

The result has been that we have been able to develop the type of critical connections—of both ideas and people—that are the essential ingredients of building a movement. The best metaphor Detroit Summer has come up with to characterize itself is "planting seeds of Hope." It is important that you be able to get a sense of how these seeds have begun to sprout to understand how, from the perspective of movement building and transformational organizing, Detroit Summer has had a greater impact than organizations with far more money and staff.

Detroit Summer brought us into contact with the Gardening Angels, a loose network of mainly African American southern-born elders, who planted gardens not only to produce healthier food for themselves and their neighbors but also to instill respect for Nature and process in young people. Getting starter kits of seeds and receiving tilling services from the city (through the Farm-a-Lot program started by Coleman's administration to assist resident gardeners), these elders worked closely with youth from Detroit's urban-based 4-H program, involving them in all aspects of gardening, nutrition, and food preservation. The Gardening Angels stayed active and in touch with one another mainly through the volunteer efforts of Gerald Hairston, a master gardener, former autoworker, and passionate environmentalist/intergenerationalist whose love for the Land, for oldsters, and for youngsters is all of one piece. With Gerald's help, Detroit Summer inspired countless groups and individuals all over the city to start gardens: neighborhood gardens, youth gardens, church gardens, school gardens, hospital gardens, senior Independence gardens, Wellness gardens, Hope Takes Root gardens, and Kwanzaa gardens.

Gerald also maintained close ties with the national and local black farmers movement, which spread the vital message that "we cannot free ourselves until we feed ourselves." In other words, it is only when we can provide for our own basic needs that we are empowered to make our own choices. Working in this spirit, Malik Yakini currently chairs the Detroit Black Community Food Security Network, which operates a two-acre farm in the city. His interest in food security is only one aspect of his overall goal of empowering blacks, who are the majority in Detroit but are mainly food consumers rather than producers and distributors.

Gerald made his transition in the summer of 2001. I had thought I had a good sense of the number of people who had been touched by his life. Every time he began a new project or met someone "you've got to meet," he would call or stop by. We were in meetings together all the time, at my house, at the 4-H club, the First Unitarian Universalist Church, Detroit Summer, the Boggs Center, University of Detroit Mercy, near the collective of urban farmers and activists on the Eastside's Farnsworth Street, or the F.A.R.M. (Foundation for Agricultural Resources in Michigan) garden launched by John Gruchala (a former member of the National Organization for an American Revolution) in the North Woodward neighborhood.

But as I witnessed the huge outpouring of people and testimonials at Gerald's memorial, I realized that I didn't know the half of it. Gerald spun spider webs with everyone. Whatever their age, race, ethnicity, gender, class, nationality, education or mis-education, ability or disability, they didn't remain strangers. He assumed that as human beings they were also Earthlings. Making phone calls, driving around in his friend Jim Stone's old beat-up Nissan, sharing articles and flyers, and delivering the *Michigan Citizen* newspaper, he was the Great Communicator, the Great Connector.

Gerald was the glue that caused the Gardening Angels to bond. He made sure that every spring their gardens were rototilled and that they got seeds from the city's Farm-a-Lot program. He drove them to 4-H and Detroit Summer community dinners and intergenerational dialogues and to Detroit Agricultural Network potlucks and meetings. He even chased the residents of a crack house off the residential street of one Gardening Angel by loading his truck with manure and parking it just outside the abandoned building. Their fame grew more and more as the secret to bringing our neighborhoods back to life.

Not only did he keep oldsters young, Gerald helped youngsters grow up, paying special attention to those ignored by others because their IQ was low, giving them doable tasks so that they could contribute and belong. He made gardeners out of city youth who had never soiled their hands. He worked with science teachers so that schoolchildren would not only learn science by growing their own food but also make their neighborhoods safer, healthier, and livelier. In his last months he was especially enthusiastic about the garden he had helped create at Holbrook Elementary School in a predominantly Muslim and Arab American neighborhood.

His creativity was limitless. He decorated plastic milk bottles and strung them together to form totem poles. He combined cotton and wool remnants with buttons and tinsel to create prize-winning carnival costumes. He turned tin cans into steel drums. His visionary and down-to-earth tours of Detroit were famous nationally and internationally.

Gerald was unique in that his dreams were not only in his heart and head but also in his hands. He opened up hearts and minds so that eyes could see vacant lots not as blight but as opportunities to develop urban agriculture and build a new society from the ground up. Born in the South, growing up on the Eastside of Detroit, and having worked in the factory, Gerald, like Jimmy Boggs, knew that we were suffering the agonies of a dying industrial society and were in transition to a new postindustrial partnership society where caring for each other and for the Earth would be a priority. He was a prototype of the new human being needed to create that new world. Those who came to remember Gerald made it clear that his spirit would be with us as long as there are gardeners in Detroit. As friends and strangers hugged, they also wondered how to stay connected now that Gerald's death had brought them together. We'll have to figure that out. As his brother, Rodney, put it, "We ought to see his death as the birth of new connections."

ONE THING LEADS TO ANOTHER

The new connections established both during and after Gerald's life have been profound indeed. Jimmy had helped us to envision the possibility of local enterprises (for-profit and not-for-profit) based on small-scale production, cooperation, and self-reliance, providing an alternative to heavy industry and get-rich-quick schemes like casinos. Through Gerald we discovered that southern-born elders, mainly but not only African American, were already planting gardens in their backyards and neighboring vacant lots, to grow food along with people and community, because their gardening embodied the human values of caring for young people and for each other. Soon after Gerald and I started working together, David Hacker of the Hunger Action Coalition and Carol Osborne of the East Michigan Environmental Action Council contacted us to suggest that we form a Detroit

Growers Support Group. The initial purpose was to provide technical support and financial assistance to teacher Kathy Wilkins and community agent Maxine Williams to create the Kwanzaa gardens next to the Howe Elementary School so that they could organize themselves into a cooperative and become the springboard for other co-ops.

Meanwhile, the Greater Detroit Health Council, with the support of the mayor's office, launched a program called Healthy Detroit, which included a gardening initiative. This encouraged the Detroit Growers Support Group to morph into the Detroit Agricultural Network with the goal of making agriculture, in all its variety, an integral part of Detroit's revitalization by creating an economy that puts a priority on food security for all people, on environmental restoration, and on growing people and communities. Working in partnership with the nonprofit Greening of Detroit and the Michigan State University Extension in Wayne County, the Detroit Agricultural Network further promoted the urban agricultural movement by offering educational programs on all aspects of gardening, along with workshops and classes that train community leaders in horticulture and community organizing.

Just a few minutes away from my home on the Eastside, Earthworks Garden also plays a central role in these efforts. This key outpost for urban agriculture is housed at the Capuchin Soup Kitchen, where the poor, homeless, ex-prisoners, and addicted come every day for a hot meal. Begun as a critical human needs provider during the depths of the Great Depression, the soup kitchen still works to meet the needs of thousands lacking basic provisions of life. Earthworks Garden seeks to address the root causes of social ills. Begun in the late 1990s by Brother Rick Samyn of the Capuchin Monastery, Earthworks now includes a commercial-size greenhouse and traverses an assortment of remediated vacant lots near areas previously occupied by industry. Earthworks is a movement-building organization that combines education with practical changes to promote a more organic and healthful way of living. Unsatisfied with the concept of charity, Brother Rick decided that the best community activism does not simply provide for others but teaches them how to provide for themselves. He especially became concerned about the limited food options available to inner-city children and families, citing the unforgettable story of a youngster who, when told they were going shopping to prepare for dinner, asked what gas station they planned to purchase their food from.

Through its Healthy Kids program, Earthworks connects gardening with nutritional education. The garden also convinced the government-sponsored Women, Infants, and Children (WIC) program to allow low-income households to use their vouchers to purchase organic Earthworks produce, and it further developed a program to market fresh vegetables at churches in the community after the Sunday service. Offering new ways to conceptualize production and consumption, the Earthworks garden grew and sold ten thousand pounds of vegetables in 2005.

On the west side of town, in one of the city's most abandoned neighborhoods littered with shuttered factories, Gerald helped connect us with the Catherine Ferguson Academy (CFA), a public high school for teenage mothers, with a nursery for their infants. Gerald had instantly bonded with Paul Weertz, a science teacher at CFA, when he spotted him riding through a vacant lot on a tractor. Working with CFA's principal, Asenath Andrews, Weertz helped to develop a life-affirming curriculum for pregnant and parenting teenagers, mostly African American. Like other urban agricultural pioneers in the city, he started on a very small scale. Weertz realized that the formaldehyde-soaked specimens typically used in biology classes would be toxic to the pregnant and nursing young women. His response was to bring in living beings that could serve as subjects for a slew of educational topics. So CFA students now learn science by running a fully functioning on-site farm with a community garden, fruit orchard, bees, and horses, as well as ducks, goats, and chickens that provide eggs and meat for the school community. They learn physics by building and raising their own barn on the school site. And most notably, the school is remarkably successful, graduating an overwhelming majority of teenage mothers, considered most at risk of dropping out, and sending nearly all of them to college.

CFA's innovative school has garnered worldwide attention. For instance, in April 2005 Marjetica Potrc, a Slovenian artist/architect who creates visionary and practical solutions for communities around the world, came to CFA to oversee a project sponsored by the Nobel Peace Center and designed by Philip Holdom of Alternative Power Solutions. CFA students assembled two small wind turbines and solar panels and climbed a twenty-five-foot scaffolding to install them on the roof of their red barn.

A video documenting the CFA installation was then presented at the Nobel Peace Center in Oslo, Norway, for a program tying CFA to the Barefoot College in Tilonia, Rajesthan, India. The Barefoot College was founded in 1972 with the conviction that solutions to rural problems lie within the community. In the Gandhian tradition, the college encourages practical knowledge and skills rather than paper qualifications and serves a population of over 125,000 people in immediate as well as distant areas. Built entirely by local people, the campus, spreading over eighty thousand square feet, runs entirely on solar electricity and houses a 700,000-liter tank for rainwater harvesting. Like the CFA installation and the Barefoot College, Marjetica's other designs are inspiring examples of how poor urban and rural communities can address questions of immediate survival in ways that are both practical and aesthetically pleasing. They include a dry toilet in the La Vega barrio of Caracas, Venezuela, which reduces the amount of water used by residents while also providing a sustainable solution to the wastewater problem, and a roundhouse for earthquake victims in El Retiro, El Salvador, which is resistant to small earthquakes and can be built by as few as two people in ten hours.

Detroit's urban agriculture also inspired an extended residency by the architectural historian and theorist Kyong Park, who had already been widely acclaimed as the founder and director of the Storefront for Art and Architecture gallery in New York City. Moving to Detroit, Park founded the International Center for Urban Ecology (ICUE) because he sensed the potential for a new kind of architecture in our city—one he calls "the Architecture of Resurrection." Among those who participated in ICUE's initial symposium were Deborah Grotfeldt, cofounder of the award-winning Project Row Houses—an organization that combines the creative arts with community organizing to promote inner-city revitalization in Houston, Texas—and Mel Chin, a Chinese American sculptor who is internationally known for his Revival Fields, in which plants are used to eliminate metals from brownfields.

In 1999 architectural students from Europe and the Detroit area worked with ICUE to develop urban design proposals providing new models for sustainable community development and presented them to residents of a near southeast Detroit neighborhood. Their proposals, based on surveying the neighborhood, included having residents on each block map the vacant land to determine its most beneficial use (e.g., for urban agriculture, fish farms, auto repair, or light industry); turning alleys into pedestrian walkways to connect the land and the people; and constructing infill housing to strengthen some blocks. One student proposed community-initiated methods to form clusters of high-density residency. Another student proposed that burned houses be turned into kilns to produce art. A modular tent to house a farmers' market that could be moved from block to block was also suggested. An architectural professor from Germany presented a plan to elicit rebuilding ideas from community residents, while others suggested that each neighborhood make a map of the specific skills of residents. All proposals sought to increase the self-reliance, self-determination, and sustainability of the community.

ICUE's originating mission was to encourage creative professionals to work closely with individuals and leaders in the community to extend, enable, and organize the grassroots and radical actions that have already been initiated by a number of urban pioneers and community activists, thus developing a new urban paradigm as a long-term alternative to mainstream policies in cities such as Detroit. "Detroit demonstrates the terminal stages of twentieth century urbanism," stated ICUE founders. "Here the city became factory, its workers brought in and housed like parts for the automobiles they assembled. Then, like a factory, it became obsolete and was discarded in the perpetual and illusory search for unsullied land and an unsullied work force." Characterizing Detroit as "a city whose scale of urban abandonment is unparalleled, a city which serves as a poster-child for the legacy of mass production," they simultaneously saw it as "a city in which an Architecture of Resistance can begin." "An Architecture of Resistance works at the roots of cities," concluded ICUE. "It works with the varied and viable strands of existing communities. It views cities as an ecosystem rather than a machine. It returns the maintenance and advancement of democracy to where it began: the city."[7]

In 2000 and 2001 students involved in Kyong Park's studio at the University of Detroit Mercy's School of Architecture created a vision of how a prairie-like area of two and a half square miles on the Eastside of Detroit near my house could be developed into a self-reliant community. They called this vision "Adamah," which roughly translates to "of the Earth" in Hebrew. Drawing from the work of Steve Vogel, the dean of the architectural school, they proposed unearthing Bloody Run Creek, which had been covered over and absorbed into the city's sewer system around the turn of the twentieth century, and remaking it into a canal for both recreation and irrigation. They envisioned greenhouses, grazing land, a dairy, and a vegetable farm to produce food; a tree farm, a lumber sawmill, and a shrimp farm; windmills to generate electricity; and living and work spaces within the massive structure housing the former Packard auto plant. They saw cohousing as well as individual housing, and schools that include community building as part of the curriculum. The Adamah project sponsors presented their vision on campus and in the community throughout the city, and Park subsequently shared his lessons from Detroit with audiences throughout the United States, Europe, and Asia.

As people viewed the twenty-minute Adamah video presentation you could almost feel their minds and imaginations expanding as they absorbed ideas for rebuilding their own neighborhoods. When the *Metro Times*, Detroit's alternative weekly, ran an extensive feature cover story on Adamah that highlighted the role the Boggs Center played it its conceptualization, we were flooded with calls and e-mails from people asking how they could get involved.[8] They demonstrated to us that there are many people out there ready to begin thinking differently about who we are and how we want to live. Some recommended that the government or some foundation or corporation be brought in to implement the Adamah plan immediately. But we responded that Adamah was not a project or blueprint but a vision. Not only should we not depend on some large entity to bring about these changes, but we must recognize that such projects will be transformative only when grassroots members of the community are moved to act. They must discover their own meaning of change in the process of building a movement to bring it about.

A QUIET REVOLUTION

What has developed through both conscious organizing drives and the actions of many individual residents is a significant urban agricultural movement in Detroit. All over the city there are now thousands of family gardens, more than two hundred community gardens, and dozens of school gardens. All over the city there are garden cluster centers that build relationships between gardeners living in the same area by organizing garden workdays and community meetings where participants share information on resources and how to preserve and market their produce. These clusters are providing a space for new grassroots leaders to emerge.

This movement is very clear about the tangible benefits of urban agriculture: it provides fresh nutritious food, beautifies neighborhoods, creates neighborhood social capital, advances neighborhood economic development, stabilizes communities, and provides sustainability. But it also provides concrete examples of alternative, value-oriented means of securing our livelihoods. In this regard, the urban agricultural movement in Detroit has arisen within the broader context of the emergence of the national environmental justice movement.

The web of connections we have established through our community work in Detroit has continued to expand exponentially. A stream of visitors—ranging from youth to elders, veteran activists to those just getting involved, and celebrities to everyday people—have come to visit the city to witness the birth of a revolution and spread the message beyond Detroit. Among the hundreds of people to which the Boggs Center has given historical and political tours of the city are community activists of all races, prominent academics, elected officials, and student groups studying urban issues or engaged in service-learning projects. At the same time, Detroit Summer has hosted students from schools across the nation, such as Macalester College, the University of Minnesota, Oberlin, Antioch, UC Santa Cruz, Oakland University, Wayne State, and the University of Michigan.

Our work has also attracted the attention of Fran and David Korten and the members of the Positive Futures Network, which views the effort to rebuild Detroit from the ground up in concert with the stories of the thousands of individuals and hundreds of groups and projects featured in *YES!* magazine. We all see ourselves as struggling to create alternatives to our present unsustainable and suicidal economy and culture. Through the Positive Futures Network, we met Danny Glover, who after touring the city and meeting with Detroit Summer activists, described it as an "amazing" program in which youth "practice the vision of transformation."

Every August the Detroit Agricultural Networ
a tour of community gardens. In 2007 six big bus
enough for the hundreds of people of all ethnic groups attrac...
by Detroit's mushrooming urban agricultural movement. After
the tour, a retired city planner told me that it gave her a sense
of how important community gardens are to a city. "They
reduce neighborhood blight, build self-esteem among young
people, provide them with structured activities from which they
can see results, build leadership skills, provide healthy food,
and a community base for economic development," she commented. "I see it as the 'Quiet Revolution.' It is a revolution for
self-determination taking place quietly in Detroit."[9]

This quiet revolution has been preparing Detroiters to meet
today's growing crises of global warming and spiraling food
prices. Instead of paying prices we can't afford for produce grown
on factory farms and imported from Florida and California in
gas-guzzling, carbon monoxide–releasing trucks, we can grow
our own food and not only achieve food security but grow our
souls because we are creating a new balance between necessity
and freedom. As Rebecca Solnit wrote in the July 2007 issue
of *Harper's Magazine*, "It is unfair, or at least deeply ironic, that
black people in Detroit are being forced to undertake an experiment in utopian post-urbanism that appears to be uncomfortably
similar to the sharecropping past their parents and grandparents
sought to escape. There is no moral reason why they should do
and be better than the rest of us—but there is a practical one.
They have to."[10]

Of all our American visitors, none has captured the essence
of Detroit's place at the end of the industrial epoch better than
Solnit. Like all who have been given our tour of the city, which
begins with the jarring and plentiful signs of decay, she was

moved and inspired by the sight of horses and goats grazing on the Catherine Ferguson Academy's farm, in the middle of one of the city's most devastated neighborhoods. But as she noted, it was the sight of "a pair of wild pheasants, bursting from a lush row of vegetables and flying over a cyclone fence toward a burned-out building across the street" that inspired her to see Detroit as "a stronghold of possibility"—one that offers "the hope that we can reclaim what we paved over and poisoned, that nature will not punish us, that it will welcome us home."

Solnit's article was followed by a five-page feature on Detroit's urban farming in the April 2008 issue of Oprah's *O Magazine*, titled "The Emerald City." Author Michele Owens spread the news about the unique curriculum of the Catherine Ferguson Academy, the organic produce of the Earthworks Garden, and the vital work of Gerald Hairston's mentee, Ashley Atkinson, with the Detroit Agricultural Network and Garden Resource Program. "Ultimately," wrote Owens, "gardening is a way of rewriting the meaning of Detroit's open land, from the end result of the worst urban pathologies to an expression of love on the part of individual Detroiters, from a stinging rejection by those with money and power to a stubborn insistence on Detroit's value by those without."[11]

Europeans have also taken a special interest in the fate of Detroit because many are particularly acute at sensing the contradictions that have emerged at the end of the industrial epoch. Several members of the British Parliament asked the Boggs Center to give them a tour of Detroit in 2002. Dutch filmmaker Boris Gerets came to Detroit to shoot a documentary called *Garden Stories* (2004), featuring a Detroit reemerging from capitalist collapse and a St. Petersburg trying to find its way out of communist collapse. At the invitation of Kyong

Park, Philipp Oswalt incorporated Detroit into the international Shrinking Cities project, alongside Ivanovo, Manchester/ Liverpool, and Halle/Leipzig. Sponsored and lavishly funded by the Federal Cultural Foundation of Germany between 2002 and 2005, the project examined the social, economic, and cultural challenges emanating from the common manifestation of postindustrial decline in four distinct geographic contexts. The creative responses of artists, scholars, activists, and architects have been exhibited in Detroit and around the world. Most recently, Canadian activist Avi Lewis hosted a 2009 episode of *Fault Lines* for the international audience of Al Jazeera English to search "amid the ruins of industrial capitalism" in Detroit to discover "glimpses of a more sustainable life," and British filmmaker Julien Temple offered BBC viewers a breathtaking view of Detroit's decline and rebirth in *Requiem for Detroit* (2010).

While I believe that the urban agricultural movement carries a special significance in Detroit, I do not mean to suggest that such activities are taking place only here. Indeed, urban communities across the nation, faced with the consequences of deindustrialization, have gone back to the farm. One of the most inspiring examples I have witnessed is Growing Power, a two-acre urban farm on the northwest side of Milwaukee, Wisconsin, where I attended a training session in March 2006. It was an unforgettable experience for me and the approximately seventy other participants, including youngsters and oldsters from all over the country and from many different backgrounds. For example, I was in a project-planning workshop with Wesley, a thirteen-year-old African American middle schooler from the neighborhood, and Hank, a middle-aged Puerto Rican psychiatrist interested in organizing a similar urban farm in his Rochester, New York, neighborhood.

Growing Power is a fulfillment of the vision of six-foot, seven-inch-tall Will Allen, the first African American to play basketball for the University of Miami. Raised on a farm in Maryland, Will always treasured the sense of extended family and community that he experienced as a child because his family never lacked for food and took it for granted that they should share it with those in need. So, after a pro basketball career and working in sales and sales technology with Proctor and Gamble, he decided in the early 1990s to buy a two-acre plot in Greenhouse Alley, a stretch of small farms that fed Milwaukee in the early twentieth century.

Will began with a vision—a vision of Independence, independence from poverty, from chemicals, from far-off food sources, from farming techniques that are no longer viable given our ever-dwindling supply of farmland and fossil fuels, and also from the illusion that community can exist without individuals accepting responsibility.

As a result, Growing Power has blossomed into a model food system that now includes year-round food production; sustainable energy and waste management; sales, marketing, and planning; and professional training, especially of urban youth and immigrants. Its Farm-City Market Basket Program provides a weekly basket of fresh produce grown by members of the Rainbow Farmer's Cooperative to hundreds of low-income urban residents at a reduced cost. I was especially fascinated by the Youth Corps program, which starts kids out when they are eight or nine and works with them until they go to college. Kids get what the schools don't provide. They work hard, learn how to think on their feet, and are challenged to solve problems instead of giving up and complaining when something doesn't work out immediately.

Powerfully built and radiating energy, Will is directly involved in the local project, hosting thousands of visitors to Growing Power in Milwaukee every year while he mentors and works with groups all over the country, providing on-the-site training in how to build a sustainable food system. "We're not just growing food," he declares. "We're growing communities."

While there is undoubtedly synergy between our efforts in Detroit and those advanced by others such as Growing Power, you may be wondering what impact all these different little groups are having on society. In the past, working within the Marxist-Leninist tradition, we would have tried to unite them all within one organization, to have them following one set of leaders and subscribing to one central strategy. But in the twenty-first century I have come to appreciate (in the words of authors Michael Hardt and Antonio Negri) the value of the "singularities" that compose the "multitude."[12] Our diversity is the source of our strength. We are not aiming simply to impact one election or one government. Rather, we are striving for long-term and sustainable transformation, and for that we need the wisdom that comes from many cultures, movements, and traditions.

When I think of this incredible movement that is already in motion, I feel our connection to the women in the village in India who sparked the Chipko movement by hugging the trees to keep them from being cut down by private contractors. I also feel our kinship with the Zapatistas in Chiapas, who announced to the world on January 1, 1994, that their development was going to be grounded in their own culture and not stunted by NAFTA's free market. And I think about how Detroiters can draw inspiration from these global struggles and how—just as in the ages of the CIO unions and the Motown sound—our city can also serve as a beacon of Hope.

Earlier this decade at a conference in Cologne, Germany, I met Maria Mies, the coauthor with Veronika Bennholdt-Thomsen of *The Subsistence Perspective* and the coauthor with Vandana Shiva of *Ecofeminism*, who sees our work in Detroit as part of this worldwide movement.[13] During a tea break the day after we met for the first time, we drafted a statement titled "Another World Is Necessary, Another World Is Possible, Another World Has Already Begun." That statement, in English, German, Spanish, and Finnish, is now circulating internationally.

Two decades ago, the urban agricultural movement seemed Utopian. But with shrinking supplies of fossil fuels, rising fuel prices, and global warming, it is beginning to look more and more practical. Even Detroit politicians now considers agriculture to be a pillar of the city's future. The key question is whether the vision for urban farming emanating from the grassroots will continue to be paramount.

For example, at a small meeting of the St. Ignatius community on the Eastside of Detroit following Hurricane Katrina, members were asked, "If you had your way, what would you like us to do in this neighborhood?"

In the ensuing discussion folks who had never heard of Adamah made proposals that seemed to come right out of the Adamah vision: community gardens to grow their own food; grocery stores, banks, barber, and beauty shops within walking distance; green spaces with trees; more intergenerational activities; a small neighborhood school where, instead of the old kind of schooling for jobs, children would develop responsibility for one another and for the community through a curriculum that engages them in community activities; a resource center with a community theater, artists' studios, and information about the different skills available in the neighborhood (e.g., car repair, plumbing, carpentry, tutoring).

Meanwhile, just a few blocks east of my home, Mike Wimberley and his octogenarian mother have created the Hope District, an eight-block strip that includes a huge lot with placards on which residents can post their dreams; a community garden and an orchard; weekend markets; and a Club Technology with sewing machines and computers for small business incubation.

As I witness and participate in our visionary efforts to revitalize Detroit and contrast them with the multibillion dollars' worth of megaprojects advanced by politicians and developers that involve casinos, giant stadiums, gentrification, and the Super Bowl, I am saddened by their shortsightedness. At the same time I rejoice in the energy being unleashed in the community by our human-scale programs that involve bringing the country back into the city and removing the walls between schools and communities, between generations, and between ethnic groups. And I am confident just as in the early twentieth century people came from around the world to marvel at the mass production lines pioneered by Henry Ford, in the twenty-first century they will be coming to marvel at the thriving neighborhoods that are the fruit of our visionary programs.

My hope is that as more and different layers of the American people are subjected to economic and political strains and as recurrent disasters force us to recognize our role in begetting these disasters, a growing number of Americans will begin to recognize that we are at one of those great turning points in history. Both for our livelihood and for our humanity we need to see progress not in terms of "having more" but in terms of growing our souls by creating community, mutual self-sufficiency, and cooperative relations with one another.

Living at the margins of the postindustrial capitalist order, we in Detroit are faced with a stark choice of how to devote ourselves to struggle. Should we strain to squeeze the last drops of life out of a failing, deteriorating, and unjust system? Or should we instead devote our creative and collective energies toward envisioning and building a radically different form of living?

That is what revolutions are about. They are about creating a new society in the places and spaces left vacant by the disintegration of the old; about evolving to a higher Humanity, not higher buildings; about Love of one another and of the Earth, not Hate; about Hope, not Despair; about saying YES to Life and NO to War; about becoming the change we want to see in the world.

CHAPTER FIVE

A Paradigm Shift in Our Concept of Education

In the spring of 2006 Oprah Winfrey devoted two full shows to our failing schools. On both shows she was joined by Microsoft billionaire Bill Gates and his wife, Melinda, who have pledged millions of dollars to address the problems of education.

"It is going to take activism," Oprah insisted. "We can't just sit passively by and act like it's OK."

She began by exposing the glaring inequities in our public schools, contrasting an inner-city Chicago school that lacks even minimal toilet facilities with a suburban school that enjoys an Olympic-size swimming pool. Again and again she cited dropout figures. One million teenagers drop out every year—not only in the inner city but also across the nation. And she pointed out that the ranks of dropouts include scores of whites. A citizen in Shelbyville, Indiana, described the local, mostly white, state-of-the-art high school as a "dropout factory."

The main reason for our failing schools, Oprah said, is that in 2006 we are still stuck with a 1956 model. Bill Gates called our school system "obsolete."

I agree. But we need a lot more dialogue on what we mean by "obsolete."

By "obsolete" Oprah and the Gateses apparently mean that our schools are falling behind those of other nations in providing the high-level skills needed to compete in today's global economy. For example, Oprah pointed out, inner-city high school seniors study eighth-grade math.

By "obsolete" I mean that the teaching and learning methods created for the age of industrialization and entrenched in our public schools no longer work in our postindustrial society.

We need much more than "reform." We need a *paradigm shift* in our concept of education. We must view the movement to transform our schools as just as vital to our twenty-first-century humanity as the civil rights movement was to our twentieth-century humanity. That is how we must approach our investment in the future. That is how we must demonstrate our love for young people and their creative capacities.

BEYOND THE FACTORY MODEL OF EDUCATION

Our failing schools have been troubling me for decades.

In the early to mid-1960s I taught in the Detroit public schools and was heavily involved in the Black Power movement and the campaign for community control of schools. But after the 1967 rebellion, I decided that the problem was not one of power and control. Rather, the time had come for a profound change in our whole concept of education. So, in 1969 I made a speech on education that has been widely reprinted, including within a collection of the Harvard Educational Review and also as a pamphlet titled *Education to Govern* that went through three printings.[1]

In that speech I warned that the youth rebellions breaking out all over the country were challenging us to go beyond community control of schools and begin grappling with fundamental questions about the purpose of education and how children learn.

At the core of the problem is an obsolete factory model of schooling that sorts, tracks, tests, and rejects or certifies working-class children as if they were products on an assembly line. The purpose of education, I said, cannot be only to increase the earning power of the individual or to supply workers for the ever-changing slots of the corporate machine. Children need to be given a sense of the "unique capacity of human beings to shape and create reality in accordance with conscious purposes and plans."

Especially in this age of rapid social and technical change, education "is not something you can make people do in their heads" with the perspective that years from now, eventually, they will be able to get a good job and make a lot of money. Some children may accept this regimen. But in a world where kids and adults watch and hear the same devastating news on TV and radio hour after hour, we can no longer treat children and young people like cogs whose "job" is to ingest basics to fit into the economic machine as workers and consumers. Those who feel most acutely the contradiction between the need for change in their daily lives and the abstractness of school subjects will create so much turmoil inside and outside the school that teachers can't teach and no one can learn.

That is why I said four decades ago that our schools must be transformed to provide children with ongoing opportunities to exercise their resourcefulness to solve the real problems of their communities. With younger children emulating older ones and older children teaching younger ones, they can learn to work together rather than competitively and experience the intrinsic consequences of their own actions. Children will be motivated to learn because their hearts, hands, and heads are engaged in improving their daily lives.

Since 1969 our neighborhoods in Detroit and other Rust Belt cities have deteriorated far beyond anything that I could possibly have imagined because our schools have continued to operate on the model created over a century ago to prepare the great majority of working-class kids for jobs on the assembly line. There once was a time when young people could drop out of school in the ninth grade and get a job in the factory, making enough money to get married and raise a family. But as robots have replaced workers on assembly lines and global corporations have been exporting jobs overseas, school dropouts have become participants in a drug economy that has turned our communities into war zones, where we live behind barred windows and triple-locked doors. Metal detectors and security guards may be able to keep guns and knives out of school buildings, but they cannot keep the chaos that disrupts our communities and the lives of our children out of our classrooms.

In cities all over the country, politicians, school boards, and administrators have come up with all sorts of palliatives masked as "reform." Their mind-set is that of controllers and enforcers. Every couple of years, school superintendents have been replaced with new more military-minded ones deemed efficiency experts. Privatization has been tried in some cities. In other cities like Detroit, the state appointed school boards to replace elected ones.

With the advent of Bush's No Child Left Behind, testing has become more frequent and more punitive, forcing teachers to teach to a sterile and often meaningless test, suppressing the creativity of committed teachers. A lot of parents have gone along because they see no alternative. Their hope is that the enforcers will at least provide an orderly school environment so that their children can get a "quality education," by which they mean the kind of education that will enable them to get a good job in the corporate structure and escape from our deteriorating neighborhoods. But as the chaos spreads, an increasing number of these parents are sending their children to magnet, charter, and private schools, thus guaranteeing that those left behind will be treated little better than prisoners with their teachers serving as little better than wardens.

President Obama has sought to prioritize educational reform by making it a focus of his economic stimulus funding. However, the selection of Arne Duncan as secretary of education means that real change, as Obama said repeatedly during the campaign, will most likely have to come from below. As CEO of Chicago Public Schools, Duncan succeeded in raising test scores slightly, but his approach to education is essentially that of the factory manager.

We need to understand that the "command and control" model has become obsolete in the wake of the information revolution, as Alvin Toffler wrote convincingly in his widely discussed 1980 book, *The Third Wave.*[2] The industrial culture of Standardization, Specialization, Centralization, Concentration, and Maximization, Toffler said, has exhausted itself. Therefore, in every area of our lives we now have the opportunity and necessity to create new decentralized institutions based on the possibilities opened up by the information revolution, for smaller work units, closer ties between producers and consumers, and greater participation in community life.

These conditions of postindustrial society especially challenge educators to reexamine conventional assumptions and to create a new community-based, person-centered model of education. Schools need to leave behind present methods geared to producing workers for highly repetitive work. They should instead seek to incorporate learning into work, political organizing, community service, and recreation. More learning needs to occur outside the classroom. Education should involve real problem solving. Instead of rigid age segregation, young and old should mingle. The years of compulsory education should grow shorter, not longer. Education should be spread out over a lifetime.

But most educators, especially the career bureaucrats of the Bush administration who forced No Child Left Behind down the throats of communities across the nation, are unwilling or unable to accept this challenge. Instead, in the name of "strict accountability," they propose punitive measures to take funds away from low-testing public schools and give them in the form of vouchers to untested private schools. Most Democrats oppose vouchers, but they are just as stuck in the dinosaur factory model.

In recent years, Toffler's views have been confirmed by educators such as Renate and Geoffrey Caine, who project a new paradigm based on the complex, creative, and self-correcting potential of the human brain. Every parent, teacher, and administrator could benefit from reading their two books, *Making Connections: Teaching and the Human Brain* (1991) and *Education on the Edge of Possibility* (1997), both published by the Association for Supervision and Curriculum Development. They believe that an education that gives children the freedom to exercise their powers creates the kind of socially responsible, visionary, and creative young people that we urgently need as change agents in the daily lives of our communities.[3]

Today's schools fail, the Caines explain, because they concentrate only on memorization instead of building on the multiple and complex powers of the human brain. Among these are the capacity to function on many levels simultaneously, to change in response to others, to keep searching for meaning, to create patterns, to enrich ideas by linking them to emotions and all the senses, to perceive and create at the same time, to be uninhibited by threats (like rewards and punishment), and to be enhanced by challenges and opportunities to make a difference.

The Caines deplore the way that factory-type schools waste this human potential because they ignore the inner and community life of students and deprive learning of meaningful context. Just as factories have been structured to produce identical/measurable parts, the Caines write, schools are organized to produce graduates who can feed back information on tests—as if the most crucial aspect of education is informational content. They are highly critical of the way schools fragment learning into subject areas while implementing measures of control—measures that repress the natural desires of children to learn and constrict naturally active young people within a confined assembly-line environment.

Schooling that denies children and young people the right to exercise these capacities produces individuals who are in a constant state of rebellion. At the same time, the Caines point out that the formal education system widens the gulf between the generations by destroying opportunities for students to learn from their elders, from their peers, and from younger children. These rebellious youth are perceived by the adult world (especially the police) as threats to an orderly society.

We all know kids who are as smart as a whip but who do poorly in school and drop out as soon as they can because they refuse to accept this violence to their humanity. I view the struggle against this obsolete, hierarchical model of education as a struggle for democracy by and for young people. The factory-type school is based on the profoundly antidemocratic belief that only experts are capable of creating knowledge, which teachers then deliver in the form of information and students give back on tests. Like workers in the factory, children and young people are denied their full humanity by a system that trains them to survive, consume, and produce.

Why do educators still practice the "command and control" model? Because in large measure it became synonymous with education in the United States. The factory model worked fairly well in the first half of the twentieth century when this country was pioneering mass production. Its limitations did not become glaring until the 1960s when we began to move toward a postindustrial society at the same time that young people, through rebellions on campus and in the streets, proclaimed their right to be full participants in deciding this country's direction.

Since then, our schools have been in continuing crisis because so few educators are able or willing to take the risk of leaving behind the old factory model and creating a new one that meets the human and social needs of young people to be creators of knowledge and of social change. Parents have not been much help because their fears for their children's survival have led them to stress staying in school to get a job. So millions of young people, coming of age in a new world where information is everywhere and industrial work is disappearing, experience schooling as senseless, a denial of their humanity and a kind of incarceration. It is because our schools are so wasteful of the creativity of our children that we have become so dependent on Ritalin and are assigning so many children to Special Ed.

Nevertheless, to keep the multibillion-dollar educational-industrial complex of publishers, administrators, teachers, construction workers, and custodians operating, we try to keep young people warehoused in schools for twelve years and more. So half of our inner-city youth routinely drop out or walk out of schools because they are no longer willing to sit passively in classrooms for twelve or more years, receiving and regurgitating information, when all around them the need for change and for creative thinking is so obvious. Having dropped out of school, most of them have no positive social role to play. So, by the hundreds of thousands, they become trapped in petty crime and the drug economy, turning our communities into hoods and ending up in prison, not only breaking up families but creating the largest prison-industrial complex in the world.

At the same time, because of a continuing decline in public school enrollments, each of which represents in Michigan the loss of approximately seven thousand dollars in state funding, our schools are in desperate financial straits. In Detroit, the dropout rate has been steadily increasing. Between 2001 and 2003, we lost about 3,000 students per year. Between 2003 and 2004, the number doubled to 6,600. Recently, the decline in Detroit public schools enrollment surpassed 9,000 students a year. As a result, our school system and our city have confronted rising, intractable budget deficits. Roughly two hundred schools have been closed in the past decade, devastating communities as well as students.

COMMUNITY-BASED EDUCATION

We are not going to solve the crisis of public education with more money, more computers, new buildings, or new CEOs. To begin with, we need the incentive that comes from recognizing how many of our children have already left it behind. We also need to go beyond struggling about who's in charge or who's to blame and recognize how the economic crisis, the urban crisis, and the education crisis are all interconnected. At this point, to develop the minds of our children we need to provide them with opportunities to discover the intrinsic relationship between effort and results through constructive participation in the life of the community along the lines projected by John Dewey.

I cannot understand why so many undergraduate students preparing to become teachers have never read or even heard of John Dewey (1859–1952)—the American pragmatist whose writings on philosophy led me from the ivory tower to the world of grassroots activism. Dewey was a pioneering educational theorist/ activist whose name is still largely synonymous with progressive education. "The tragic weakness of the present school," Dewey said, "is that it endeavors to prepare future members of the social order in a medium in which the conditions of the social spirit are eminently wanting." He condemned teaching that focuses on "the mere absorption of facts and truths" done as such "an exclusively individual an affair that it tends very naturally to pass into selfishness." By contrast, Dewey argued that "where active work is going on, all this is changed" and "a spirit of free communication, of interchange of ideas, [and] of suggestions results."[4]

Because Dewey insisted that education is "a process of living and not a preparation for future living," he called for the school to "represent present life—life as real and vital to the child as that which he carries on in the home, in the neighborhood or on the playground." "Our present education," he said, "is highly specialized, one-sided and narrow. It is an education dominated almost entirely by the medieval conception of learning. It is something which appeals for the most part simply to the intellectual aspects of our natures, our desire to learn, to accumulate information, and to get control of the symbols of learning; not to our impulses and tendencies to make, to do, to create, to produce, whether in the form of utility or of art."[5]

Even the way we organize our classrooms robs children of creativity and initiative. "Rows of ugly desks placed in geometrical order, crowded together so that there shall be as little moving room as possible . . . are all made 'for listening'—for simply studying lessons out of a book is only another kind of listening; it marks the dependency of one mind over another." This "attitude of listening"—guided by the expectation that the child will take in "certain ready-made materials" that have been prepared by his or her superiors—ultimately promotes "passivity."

"From the standpoint of the child," Dewey concluded, "the great waste in the school comes from his inability to utilize the experience he gets outside the school in any complete and free way within the school itself; while, on the other hand, he is unable to apply in daily life what he is learning in school. That is the isolation of the school—its isolation from life."[6]

While Dewey was challenging the U.S. model of education, Mahatma Gandhi was forced to address the colonial mind-set that developed under British rule in India. During the struggle for independence, Gandhi recognized that the educational system was "meant for strengthening and perpetuating the imperialist power in India." It had been designed to supply the next generation of clerks to sign, stamp, and file the paperwork to run the British Empire. As a result, most elite Indian students found manual work "irksome." However, he retorted, the development of a true intellect necessitated the balanced and "harmonious growth of body, mind and soul." "That is why we give manual labour the central place in our curriculum of training here," Gandhi remarked in a teachers' training camp. "An intellect that is developed through the medium of socially useful labour will be an instrument for service and will not easily be led astray or fall into devious paths."[7]

Against the system of education set up to serve British interests, Gandhi proposed a system of popular education to serve the Indian people. He especially focused on the villages, where the vast majority of the people lived and were left untouched, seen only as suppliers of cheap raw materials for the British or as potential markets for the finished goods the British wanted to sell them. Teach people what will truly help them, he said, not to become servants and bureaucrats for the Empire but to aid them in all the little things of village life. Education, he said, should be of the Heart, the Hand, and the Head. It should give people an understanding of themselves and where they stand in the world and, from there, their obligations toward their neighbor. The three main resources for this popular education, he said, are the community, the natural environment, and the world environment.

Although Dewey and Gandhi were two of the great thinkers of their time, their passings in the mid-twentieth century precluded their witnessing the new social movements of the 1960s and developing a response to the intensified crises of our inner cities. That is why I was fortunate to come into contact with Paulo Freire's ideas in 1970, when my late husband, Jimmy Boggs, and I were struggling to clarify the distinction between rebellion and revolution in the wake of the urban explosions of 1967 and 1968.

Freire was born in 1921 and died in 1997, before the dawn of the new millennium. His ideas and actions have reverberated with teachers and grassroots organizers around the world and have particularly helped to reshape the political landscape of his native Brazil. The power of Freire's ideas is always with me. Whenever I am evaluating a revolutionary strategy or trying to devise one, I find myself recalling his insights, for example, people "cannot enter the struggle as objects in order *later* to become human beings" or "The future isn't something hidden in a corner. The future is something we build in the present."

I first encountered Freire's writings through a little pamphlet called *Cultural Action for Freedom*. In this pamphlet, he used the phrase "naive transitivity" to describe what we and other movement activists in the 1960s were calling "rebellion." For Freire, it was the stage when the masses, conscious that their oppression is rooted in objective conditions, "become anxious for freedom, anxious to overcome the silence in which they have always existed." Freire was very clear, as were we, that this breaking of silence was not just a riot. Indeed, the masses were seeking to make their historical presence felt. He was equally clear, as were we, that it was not yet revolution because revolutions are made by people (as distinguished from masses) who have assumed "the role of subject in the precarious adventure of transforming and re-creating the world. They are not just denouncing but also announcing a new positive."[8] Or as we put it in *Revolution and Evolution in the Twentieth Century*, "a rebellion disrupts the society," but "a revolution . . . begins with projecting the notion of a more human, human being," one "who is more advanced in the qualities which only human beings have—creativity, consciousness and self-consciousness, a sense of political and social responsibility."[9]

Soon thereafter, I read Freire's *Pedagogy of the Oppressed* and was delighted to discover that his ideas of Education for Freedom, as education that not only makes the masses conscious of their oppression but engages them in struggles to transform themselves and their world, were very close to those that I had been putting forward.[10] In this landmark work, Freire critiqued the bourgeois "banking method" of education, in which students are expected to memorize the "truths" of the dominant society—that is, "deposit" information in their head then "withdraw" it when required for tests, jobs, and other demands by overseers. Instead, Freire argued that critical thinking can develop only when questions are posed as problems. This problem-posing method provides no automatic "correct" answer. By contrast, students must discover their own understanding of the truth by developing a heightened awareness of their situation.

Freire's revolutionary method of education has also transformed the way we approach political organizing and struggle, for as he maintained, we must view making revolution as an inherently educational process. Freire argued that revolutionary work must transform the oppressed from passive victims to agents of history, seeking "the pursuit of fuller humanity." Thus, the emphasis is on people taking control of their own destiny—"self-determination" in the truest sense of the word. Transforming relations means that revolution is not about the oppressed switching places with the oppressors, nor is it about the "have-nots" acquiring the material possessions of the "haves." It is about overcoming the "dehumanization" that has been fostered by the commodification of everything under capitalism and building more democratic, just, and nourishing modes of relating to people. Critical of the Marxist-Leninist and nationalist parties that had led most of the anticapitalist and anticolonial movements around the world, Freire insisted that what was needed to revolutionize society was not a narrow focus on seizing state power but a cultural revolution in the form of a continuous struggle to transform human relations.

Today, in the United States, if we substitute our cities for the villages of Gandhi's India or the favelas of Freire's Brazil, we are at a similar crossroads. Our educational system has been set up to supply the next generation of technicians and bureaucrats for the global economy, an economy that is fundamentally undemocratic because it destroys our communities, robs us of control over our daily lives, and reduces us to passive consumers. Instead of viewing the purpose of education as giving students the means for upward mobility or helping the United States to compete on the world market, we need to recognize that the aptitudes and attitudes of people with BAs, BSs, MBAs, and PhDs bear a lot of the responsibility for our planetary and social problems. Formal education bears a large part of the responsibility for our present crisis because it produces morally sterile technicians who have more know-*how* than know-*why*. At a time when we desperately need to heal the Earth and build durable economies and healthy communities, too many of our schools and universities are stuck in the processes and practices used to industrialize the Earth in the nineteenth and twentieth centuries.

We can't change the whole system overnight. But we need to know what we would put in its place, and we can take advantage of the present crisis to begin working to create new models with the teachers, principals, and parents all over the city who have given themselves permission to think differently from the powers-that-be. To achieve the miracle that is now needed to transform our schools into places of learning, we need to tap into the creative energies of our children and our teachers.

In this connection, we have much to learn from the struggles in Alabama and Mississippi in the early 1960s.

In the spring of 1963 the Southern Christian Leadership Conference led by Dr. King launched a "fill the jails" campaign to desegregate downtown department stores and schools in Birmingham. But few local blacks were coming forward. Black adults were afraid of losing their jobs, local black preachers were reluctant to accept the leadership of an "Outsider," and city police commissioner Bull Connor had everyone intimidated. Facing a major defeat, King was persuaded by his aide, James Bevel, to allow any child old enough to belong to a church to march. So on D-day, May 2, before the eyes of the whole nation, thousands of schoolchildren, many of them first graders, joined the movement and were beaten, fire-hosed, attacked by police dogs, and herded off to jail in paddy wagons and school buses. The result was what has been called the "Children's Miracle." Inspired and shamed into action, thousands of adults rushed to join the movement. All over the country rallies were called to express outrage against Bull Connor's brutality. Locally, the power structure was forced to desegregate lunch counters and dressing rooms in downtown stores, hire blacks to work downtown, and begin desegregating the schools. Nationally, the Kennedy administration, which had been trying not to alienate white Dixiecrat voters, was forced to begin drafting civil rights legislation as the only way to forestall more Birminghams.

The next year as part of Mississippi Freedom Summer, activists created Freedom Schools because the existing school system (like ours today) had been organized to produce subjects, not citizens. People in the community, both children and adults, needed to be empowered to exercise their civil and voting rights. A mental revolution was needed. To bring it about, reading, writing, and speaking skills were taught through discussions of black history, the power structure, and building a movement. Everyone took this revolutionary civics course, then chose from more academic subjects such as algebra and chemistry. All over Mississippi, in church basements and parish halls, on shady lawns and in abandoned buildings, volunteer teachers empowered thousands of children and adults through this community curriculum.

The Freedom Schools of 1964 demonstrated that when Education involves young people in making community changes that matter to them, when it gives meaning to their lives in the present instead of preparing them only to make a living in the future, young people begin to believe in themselves and to dream of the future. As they engage in these meaningful activities, they also begin expressing themselves in meaningful language that is appropriate to the activities in which they are engaged. Thus, the most popular subjects among Mississippi Freedom Schoolers were foreign languages, poetry, and drama. Thus, also, Detroit Summer has given birth to some remarkable young poets who have created year-round poetry workshops for social change and a media center, where young people are exploring new ways of creating community through new ways of meaningful communication.

THE FUTURE OF EDUCATION

Just as in 1963 and 1964, when the creative energies of children and young people were tapped to win the battle for desegregation and voting rights, today they need to be tapped to rebuild our communities and to create a vibrant society and a democratic citizenry.

To understand the current crisis of education and project a better future for our children, we need to begin thinking about how our culture is shaped by the means through which we communicate: the spoken word, the printed word, and the images of the electronic media. No one understood this better than the late Neil Postman, the New York University professor who wrote more than a dozen fascinating books on education and communication. At the end of the 1960s I read his first book, *Teaching as a Subversive Activity*, coauthored with Charles Weingartner.[11] It had a big influence on me when I was writing *Education to Govern*.

In *The Disappearance of Childhood*, first published in 1982, Postman explained that childhood is a cultural artifact that did not exist before the invention of the printing press in the fifteenth century. In the medieval world, when people communicated mainly through the spoken word, children participated in adult activities and became part of the adult world at the age of seven when they were able to follow adult conversations. However, the printing press ushered in an explosion of books and of individualism because reading is a private activity. Individuals reading the Bible on their own gave birth to the Protestant Reformation. Widespread reading also gave birth to the idea of childhood as a period of preparation for adulthood, a period during which the child acquires literacy through a rigorous step-by-step process, at the same time developing beyond immediate gratification and toward self-control and the ability to analyze.

The school emerged as the place within which this civilizing process takes place under the tutelage of adults. Thus, the concepts of childhood and schooling were essentially hierarchical. Originally schools were mainly for the middle classes. Poor children and children of color worked in the fields, mines, and mills and gained access to public schooling only through heroic struggles. The hundred years between 1850 and 1950 were preoccupied with these struggles. In 1899 these concepts of childhood and schooling were challenged in two landmark books: Freud's *Civilization and Its Discontents* and John Dewey's *The School and Society.* Freud warned that society could not afford to ignore the natural instincts of children. Dewey argued against schooling only as a preparation for life in the future. During their school years, he insisted, children need to be constructive participants in the social life of the community.[12]

Meanwhile, a new method of communication, the telegraph, had been invented. The telegraph made it possible to send and receive an unlimited amount of decontextualized information from everywhere, 24/7, thus changing the character of information from the personal and regional to the impersonal and global. Since then, the electronic media have wrested control of information from the home and from the school, reaching its peak in TV, a form of communication as different from the printed word as the printed word was from the spoken word. TV is a present-centered medium that cannot give a sense of past or future. Because it involves perception, not conception, it makes no complex demands on and requires no skills of viewers.[13]

By the time the average American child goes to school, s/he has watched thousands of hours of television. As a result, most children from nonintellectual homes resist the rigorous, linear, hierarchical kind of schooling that was created during the centuries when the main means of communication was the printed word. As Ruby Dee put it, "Their minds have been sucked out through their eyeballs."

restore their minds by trying to restore the kinds
at were an outgrowth of the print culture. Instead,
appreciate that today's youth have been born and
the new information technology of the Web. George
Siemens, the Canadian educator, argues that this new information technology has already transformed the way that young
people communicate and learn: horizontally rather than verti-
cally, collectively and collaboratively rather than individually
and competitively. Siemens recommends that educators celebrate local excellence and innovations, let people teach each
other, and allow students to organize themselves. Education, in
other words, serves as a model democracy.[14]

Through Detroit Summer, a new generation of youth activists is using the new information technology to engage students
in grappling with the deepening crisis in our schools. Detroit
Summer Collective members Ilana Weaver (an independent
artist/rapper who performs as "Invincible") and Jenny Lee
describe how the Live Arts Media Project serves as a democratic
model of Freedom Schooling:

> In the summer of 2006, Detroit Summer launched a campaign to
> transform the entire education system in Detroit, inspired by several
> young people we worked with who had dropped out, or were con-
> sidering dropping out, as well as some who were organizing in their
> schools for a change but were suspended or arrested as a result.
> After attending several community forums on the issue we noticed
> a glaring piece was missing; no one was asking youth, the people
> most impacted by the schools crisis, what they thought. There were
> fingers pointed but no long-term sustainable solutions proposed.
> We realized that we needed to evolve the whole concept of what
> it meant to campaign for social change. What would happen if we
> explored the question of why people drop out as a community,
> in order to generate solutions as a community, while prioritizing

the voices of youth? And what if, instead of a standard campaign 12-point platform, we created a Hip-Hop audio documentary to express our demands? And what if we didn't just critique the outdated teaching methods that are in place, but also modeled the process of hands-on real life learning? We launched the Live Arts Media Project (LAMP) as an answer to all those questions and an experiment in a different type of community organizing.

We've found that the model of Hip-Hop–based community organizing, developed through the Live Arts Media Project, is useful to people in many different places, facing similar crises as Detroit. Since the completion of our first Hip-Hop audio documentary, entitled *Rising Up from the Ashes: Chronicles of a Dropout*, LAMP youth and artist mentors have traveled around the Midwest, California, and as far as Deheishe Refugee Camp in the West Bank, Palestine, exchanging models with other youth leadership projects.

Last year I witnessed a demonstration of the effectiveness of this horizontal teaching/learning process at a workshop conducted for about forty high school students by Starlet and Kendra, two high school members of the Detroit Summer Collective. They handed out sheets of paper and asked participants to fold them into four boxes. In the upper left-hand box they were asked to write "school crisis"; in the upper right-hand box, "individual solution"; in the lower left-hand box, "community solution"; and in the lower right-hand box, "national solution." Each participant then handed the sheet to the person on the right to fill in. The general discussion that followed was both moving and enlightening, and the forty young participants agreed to take the process back to their high schools.

We need more schools and programs that place a horizontal teaching/learning process at the center of a community-building model of education. One example created by public schools in the deindustrialized cities of New England is a program called KIDS: Kids Involved in Doing Service. Students at the Moretown Elementary School in Vermont, for example, researched the feasibility of planting trees along the banks of the Mad River to decrease thermal impact on the river, absorb runoff, and enhance animal habitats. Middle school students in Bath, Maine, mapped a historical walking tour of downtown Bath for distribution by the chamber of commerce, local restaurants, and information centers. Lewiston Middle School students restored the interior and exterior appearance of their historic building.

Over a decade ago, the Pew Charitable Trust, recognizing the overwhelming desire of young people to act on behalf of the environment and to help their communities through voluntary service, created Earth Force, a program that helps schoolchildren monitor water quality and solve other environmental problems in their communities.

In Ypsilanti, Michigan, there is a nonprofit organization calling itself Creative Change Educational Solutions (CCES), which provides teachers with training and curricula designed to make connections among the environment, society, and the economy. The lessons are aligned with national and state standards and can be easily integrated into economics, civics, language, or science classes. Teachers who have been trained by CCES talk about how exciting it is to teach in this way. Test scores rise because the kids see themselves in the hands-on projects. For example, clean air really means something to them because many use inhalers. Instead of depending on teachers to choose the lessons, the kids bring lessons to the teachers based on their own experiences.

There may be similar models in other parts of the country. But the importance of programs such as Detroit Summer, KIDS, Earth Force, and CCES is that, by enlisting the energies and creativity of schoolchildren in addressing the urban crisis, they provide children and young people with opportunities to take ownership of problems or issues affecting their school and their town. Thereby, they give meaning to the lives of our children in the present while preparing them to become active citizens in a democratic society. At the same time, they foster the culture of hope and change in the community, which is something we all need, whether we live in the inner city or the suburbs.

In the last two years of his life, Dr. Martin Luther King Jr. was anticipating this kind of Freedom Schooling when he deplored the way educators were trying to instill white, middle-class values in black youth. King called for programs to involve young people in direct actions "in our dying cities" that would be "self-transforming and structure-transforming."

This is the kind of Freedom Schooling we need today. Schools and colleges dedicated to this new approach—one far more visionary than the generic call for access to "quality education"—would look and act differently from today's educational institutions. That is why we must go beyond slogans like "Education, Not Incarceration" and begin exploring new forms of community-based, person-centered Freedom Schooling. What we urgently need are school boards, school superintendents and college presidents, teachers and parents with the imagination and courage to introduce innovative curriculums and structures. We need to create a much more intimate connection between intellectual development and practical activity, to root students and faculty in their communities and natural habitats, and to engage them in the kind of real problem solving in their localities that nurtures a love of place and provides practice in creating the sustainable economies, equality, and community that are the responsibilities of citizenship.

Just imagine what our neighborhoods would be like if, instead of keeping our children isolated in classrooms for twelve years and more, we engaged them in community-building activities with the same audacity with which the civil rights movement engaged them in desegregation activities fifty years ago! Just imagine how safe and lively our streets would be if, as a natural and normal part of the curriculum from K–12, schoolchildren were taking responsibility for maintaining neighborhood streets, planting community gardens, recycling waste, rehabbing houses, creating healthier school lunches, visiting and doing errands for the elderly, organizing neighborhood festivals, and painting public murals!

The possibilities are endless. Our children will be absorbing naturally and normally the values of social responsibility and cooperation at the same time that they are being inspired to learn the skills and acquire the information necessary to solve real problems. This is the fastest way to motivate all our children to learn and at the same time turn our communities, almost overnight, into lively neighborhoods where crime is going down because hope is going up. It is something needed not only by children in cities such as Detroit but in suburbs and exurbs like Littleton, Colorado—site of the Columbine High School massacre.

CHAPTER SIX

We Are the Leaders We've Been Looking For

Several years ago I received a poster of a twenty-something me designed by New Mexico artist Amy Gerber, whom I've never met. Amy created the poster after she heard me say on *Bill Moyers Journal* in June 2007 that "we need to embrace the idea that we are the leaders we've been looking for."

The phrase comes from the story that Zoharah Simmons, now a University of Florida professor of religion, tells of her experience four decades ago. As a very young and somewhat nervous Mississippi Freedom Summer volunteer going door to door with the Student Nonviolent Coordinating Committee, she was reassured when Mrs. Euberta Sphinks answered her knock and said, "Girl, I've been waiting for you all my life."[1]

I am reminded of Zoharah whenever I'm asked, "Where are the leaders for today's movement coming from?" It seems to me that just as most people are still thinking of revolution as the seizure of state power and instituting wholesale changes from above, our ideas of leadership have been stuck in the concept of the vanguard party created by Lenin over a century ago in a

Russia where the overwhelming majority were peasants unable to read or write and without access to daily papers, let alone to radio, TV, or the Internet.

The year 2008 represented a breakthrough, as growing numbers answered the call of Barack Obama: "We are the ones we've been waiting for." The morning after Obama's speech at the Democratic Party convention, for instance, I received a hope-filled e-mail from Rob "Biko" Baker, the young African American who is the executive director of the League of Young Voters and organizes Milwaukee youth in the Campaign against Violence. Two months earlier, I had met with Biko and League field organizers at a small dinner in Ann Arbor.

Last night, for the first time in my adult life, I waved an American Flag. It was just a little thing; a stick and fabric symbol, the same kind ancient veterans in immaculate uniforms hand out on the 4th of July. In my hand, it felt as light as air. It was something to be careful with. . . .

I waved that flag because I believe that change is finally possible in our country. For too long the people who form the bedrock of our nation have been left out of the American Dream. Our greatest leaders have been murdered and destroyed, our institutions broken. We, our friends and families, work ourselves to the bone to make ends meet and can expect each day to simply be more of the same.

After last night's historic event, I woke up convinced that we can realize our beautiful dream. It wasn't the candidate that changed me. It wasn't the speech. It was the faces of those around me showing me that we, as Americans, are sick of the status quo. We are tired of inequality. We are ready to step up to be leaders in the greatest tradition of the men and women who placed this flag, this land, into our hands.

I believe we have what it takes to tackle the contradictions that continue to divide us. We can truly become the "Change Genera-tion." We face problems unprecedented in human history, and we must meet them as brothers and sisters. We are going to have to work harder every day, to convince the skeptical, and demonstrate the power of the Beloved Community over and over again. If we want it, we can do it. Last night we proved it.[2]

It was not Obama's policy proposals (which were not that different from those of other Democrats) that inspired this fervent response from Biko. Nor was it Obama's charisma. What inspired it, I believe, was participating in and witnessing the drama of the Democrats nominating an African American for president on the forty-fifth anniversary of the 1963 March on Washington, thus demonstrating before the eyes of the world the power of grassroots organizing. Even Bill Clinton had a role in this drama. His speech not only sanctified his own presidency but also disclosed why a section of the power structure supports Obama—to improve our image in the world.

These transformative energies at the grassroots level are our best hope in this period when the government in DC has essentially become dysfunctional. It was block by block, from the ground up, community organizing that won the White House for Obama. Inspired by his eloquence and audacity, his commitment to change we can believe in, and his faith in himself and in human possibilities, and determined to leave behind us the shameful legacy of slavery, Jim Crow, the Iraq War, and the other atrocities of the Bush-Cheney regime, we began to heal and redeem our country and ourselves. Americans of all ages, ethnic backgrounds, and faiths; members of unions, churches, and synagogues; and peace, women's, and other community groups discovered in ourselves the energy that comes from renewed hope and commitment to a just cause.

So we went door-to-door in neighborhoods all over the country, persuading strangers and folks who had never voted or who had lost faith in voting, to vote for Obama. It was a great feat—one worthy of celebration. The participation of so many millions of Americans from all walks of life in the Obama campaign, their interacting with him at rallies, the tireless canvassing by volunteers, the patient waiting in long lines to cast ballots prior to and on election day—all this means that we have taken a giant step toward becoming a more responsible, more democratic, and more self-governing people.

Where do we go from here? Some people will use the experience to advance their own careers. Others will be content with Obama's closing down Guantánamo and undoing similar Bush-Cheney abuses. Still others, outraged at Obama's appointments of unyielding Zionists, right-wing Democrats, and economic heavyweights whose only concern is growing the economy, will organize protest demonstrations, trying to push Obama to the left. Or they will regret that they did not vote for Ralph Nader or Cynthia McKinney. But I see a different path ahead.

During the inauguration on January 20, 2009, I had the opportunity to talk on *Democracy Now!* with Amy Goodman, who was covering the historic event with Alice Walker.

I said that I was struck by the grimness of Obama's face as he walked to his seat on the podium. I felt a disconnect between that grimness and the jubilation of the millions awaiting his arrival. I also thought that his speech (in which he invoked past presidents) lacked the "Together We Can" energy of the campaign and the Love, the turning to one another and the legacy of past grassroots struggles that were in Elizabeth Alexander's poem and Reverend Joseph Lowery's benediction. It reflected, instead, the difficulties, complexities, burdens, and constraints of the Oval Office, and the reality that, as president and commander in chief, Barack Obama was now responsible not only for reviving a failed economic system while saddled with a trillion-dollar deficit but also extricating us from two failed wars and rescuing an obsolete school system. He must now bend to liberals, moderates, and conservatives just to pass modest health care legislation that will not make us more healthy but only make health insurance more available

And I wondered how we, the people, can bridge this disconnect.

Alice said that she was also troubled "at the weight of the responsibility that he [Obama] must be feeling, because now, after all, here he is, the president, and his word will have so much clout in the world."

"There should be some way that ordinary citizens could really show an understanding of what we are asking of this family," she added. "This is some of what has to be going through his mind as he takes on this office of president of the United States at a time when everything is falling apart."[3]

The next day, to my delight, my questions and concerns were answered by a small group of Milwaukee community activists who caravanned to DC for the inauguration and stopped on their way back to spend a few hours at the Boggs Center.

From their lively accounts of the trip, I got a sense of the range of emotions they had gone through. There was, to begin with, the excitement as they drove east (often through blizzards), meeting and greeting (on the road and at rest stops) countless others embarked on the same journey, and finally arriving in DC. Then the confusion and frustrations of getting around, each trying to find the way to and from different destinations (including porta-potties) in the midst of more than a million equally confused and frustrated out-of-towners, also trying to find their way and their group—giving rise to anger, complaints, and competition: "I've been here since 6 A.M. and you can't cut in front of me."

"But out of this chaos, community began to emerge," wrote Peggy Hong, one of the Milwaukee activists, in her blog. "A group was trying to get past us, and a young guy from California suggested that we open a channel for them to pass through so that we could also move. So eight or 10 of us coached a mile of people past our section. 'Come on through, watch your step, single file, keep moving,'" Hong said. "This spontaneous grassroots effort guided the flow, made us active instead of passive, and helped others in need."[4]

On the all-night drive home (again through blizzards) they discussed and reflected on the experience. Small groups like ours, they decided, now have the opportunity and responsibility to work in our communities to help our neighbors and fellow citizens create passageways through the chaos that now exists where we live and work. All over the country there are small groups like ours. As the crisis deepens, forcing us to look to each other to survive, our local efforts can create communities of Hope, cities of Hope, regions of Hope, and overall, a New America of Hope. This is what we need to do now.

As we talked, I was reminded of the importance of combining activity with reflection, as we enter a new period of movement. This was something we had not yet learned to do in the sixties.

Our responsibility, at this watershed in our history, is to face the past honestly and do the things necessary to heal ourselves and our planet. Healing our society will require the patient work not primarily of politicians but of artists, ministers, gardeners, workers, families, women, and communities. It will require new forms of governance, work, and education that are much more participatory and democratic than those collapsing all around us. It will require enlarging our vision and decolonizing our imaginations.

Obama can't create these new forms from the Oval Office. They can be created only at the grassroots level. I do not delude myself that he will be able to initiate the profound changes in our values, how we live, how we make our living, and how we educate our children that are urgently needed at this milestone in our evolution. We are in the midst of a cultural transition as far-reaching as that from hunting and gathering to agriculture eleven thousand years ago and from agriculture to industry three hundred years ago.

Our challenge now is to recognize that the future of our country and our planet is as much about us as about Obama, that in our communities and our cities we have become responsible for grappling with the issues he is wrestling with—the economic meltdown, our unsustainable lifestyle, the future of the U.S. auto industry, the health and education of our children, and how to extricate ourselves from our occupation of Iraq and Afghanistan and resolve the many other crises in the Middle East, Africa, Latin America, and Asia. Because we played such a huge role in electing him, because these issues are so critical to our daily lives, and because our transformation toward taking greater responsibility has been so great, we cannot return to the old separation between we, the people, and those we elect to office.

How do we continue this transformative process? How do we join in the work, calloused hand by calloused hand, of remaking this nation, block by block, brick by brick? How do we nurture this new spirit of service, sacrifice, patriotism, and responsibility, wherein each of us resolves to pitch in and work harder and look after not only ourselves but also each other?

We might begin by discussing these and related questions with our families, neighbors, coworkers, classmates, church members, Bible study groups, book clubs, garden clubs, bowling clubs, or any gathering at which we find ourselves.

Movement elder Vincent Harding, reflecting on the meaning of Obama's election, argues that we need to see ourselves as the midwives of a new America. Like Biko Baker, Harding found himself in Denver among the tens of thousands listening to Obama's acceptance speech. "It seemed obvious to me," he wrote, "that my young brother seems to offer the place where all the 'we' people can stop our waiting and carry on our work to create the pathway, the birthing channel toward 'The land that never has been yet, and yet must be.' Not only is something trying to be born in America, but some of us are called to be the midwives in this magnificent and painfully creative process."[5]

Harding reminds us that the new possibilities that are animating millions of Americans and people around the world did not spring out of thin air and they were not handed to us from above. They were potentialities that millions of us have nurtured for years. Now we must continue to care for them and help them blossom.

WHAT DOES BOTTOM-UP CHANGE LOOK LIKE?

Decades from now I hope that our grandchildren and great-grandchildren will be celebrating the first decade of the twenty-first century as the best of times because it was the decade when we, the American people, were finally forced to look in the mirror by catastrophes such as 9/11, the Iraq and Afghanistan

Wars, global warming, Hurricane Katrina, massive housing fore-closures, and the financial crisis.

It was the decade when we recognized that it "is not in our stars, but in ourselves, that we are underlings." (This quote from Shakespeare's *Julius Caesar* was a favorite of my late husband, Jimmy Boggs.)

In this decade, slowly but surely, we recognized that our catas-trophes are not acts of nature but the consequences of our own ideas and actions. Therefore, we can bring an end to them by transforming the way we have been thinking and living.

There are a variety of ways in which people, some who con-sciously consider themselves activists and others who simply view themselves as responsible members of a local neighbor-hood or citizenry, are going about community-building work. For example, the environmental justice movement represents a significant political development because it has challenged us to go beyond antiracism to develop a more holistic perspective. The environmental justice movement exposes "toxic racism," showing how harmful activities and polluting industries are found in high concentrations within low-income neighborhoods and commu-nities of color. It demands that corporations and governmental bodies be held accountable for cleaning toxic sites and maintain-ing a healthy environment where we live, work, and play.

However, at its best, the environmental justice movement refuses to be locked into a protest politics mode. Instead, it seeks to nurture a new consciousness to heal the physical and spiri-tual damage caused by decades of unchecked industrial growth. Although I didn't attend the first People of Color Environmental Summit in October 1991, out of which came the Seventeen Principles of Environmental Justice, I view these principles as no less than the foundation for a new U.S. Constitution. Every environmental action group, every class in public health, should discuss them periodically. Some of the most vital principles include

> Principle #1: Environmental Justice affirms the sacredness of Mother Earth, ecological unity and the interdependence of all species, and the right to be free from ecological destruction.
>
> Principle #7: Environmental Justice demands the right to participate as equal partners at every level of decision-making, including needs assessment, planning, implementation, enforcement and evaluation.
>
> Principle #17: Environmental Justice requires that we, as individuals, make personal and consumer choices to consume as little of Mother Earth's resources and to produce as little waste as possible; and make the conscious decision to challenge and reprioritize our lifestyles to ensure the health of the natural world for present and future generations.[6]

This is exactly the type of visionary thinking we need to be doing and practicing if we really intend to transform our world.

This means we must also realize that the massive housing foreclosures destroying whole neighborhoods are the result of the sad reality that on much of Main Street as well as Wall Street we have created a casino economy by assuming that we can live endlessly on credit. By recognizing our own culpability instead of putting all the blame on and demonizing others, we can discover the power within each of us to change the world by changing ourselves. One way to begin a new conversation, not only with Obama supporters but also with those who voted for McCain, is by providing examples of how we would be safer and happier if we lived more simply so others could simply live. What we need are not stopgap measures like the bailouts concocted by George W. Bush and his Wall Street secretary of the Treasury. What we need instead is a paradigm shift toward a solidarity economy whose foundation is the production and exchange of goods and services that our communities really need. Recently, we have seen an outburst of "Tea Party" protests denouncing "big government" as a threat to freedom while unleashing anxieties about immigration and the emerging nonwhite majority. However, carrying out the true spirit of the activists who sparked the first American Revolution in December 1773 means rejecting consumerism and the stranglehold of luxury goods on our lives. Just as the original Boston Tea Party threw overboard crates of tea on British-owned ships to declare their independence from English colonialism, we need to burn our credit cards to demonstrate our independence from the casino economy. Instead of rhetorical flourishes against "socialism," we need active and working declarations of our commitment to creating local economies based on new principles and ethics of real work.

What would this look like in practice? In a thoughtful article for *YES!* magazine, Ethan Miller, who works at a land-based mutual aid cooperative in Maine, calls for a paradigm shift in the way we think about economic development.[7] The conventional wisdom, especially promoted by politicians, is that economic development comes only from outside—in other words, from developers. In fact, our economy includes all the ways we sustain and support ourselves, our families, and our communities. What actually holds the very fabric of our society together are local activities that are not done for money: household activities such as raising children and cooking; barter activities like trading services with friends or neighbors; and cooperative enterprises based on common ownership and control. These mutual care and cooperative activities are the seeds of "another economy."

The movement toward community self-reliance and an economy rooted in human solidarity rather than amoral competition has become especially prominent in some Asian and Latin American countries. It may be hard for some to appreciate that another economy is possible in the United States—that is, within the belly of the beast. But in fact it is already emerging. Gar Alperovitz, a historian and economist who works with the Democracy Collaborative at the University of Maryland, documents this emergence in his 2004 book *America beyond Capitalism: Reclaiming Our Wealth, Our Liberty and Our Democracy*. Out of his firsthand experiences in the civil rights movement, in the anti–Vietnam War movement, and with the steelworkers in Youngstown, he has gained an understanding of how new movements can arise seemingly out of nowhere when systemic changes become necessary.

Alperovitz is deeply troubled by the downward trend of the past few decades, as Americans have been steadily becoming less equal, less free, and less able to control our own fate. However, he has also witnessed millions of Americans responding to the insecurities and suffering caused by huge multinational corporations by creating new forms of community-based institutions to give "we the people" ownership and control over the way we make our living.

Some of the notable developments documented in *America beyond Capitalism* are the following:

- In all, 130 million Americans are now involved in co-ops, mostly credit unions, and cooperative housing.

- Eleven thousand employee-owned companies already exist in this country. Together they involve more workers than the total membership in unions of private corporations.

- The number of community development corporations (CDCs) and municipally owned utilities is steadily growing.

- Since the 1960s, countless nonprofit organizations have been created to serve community needs. Most of these are funded by foundations but many support themselves by organizing local enterprises.

- The share of locally owned businesses has also increased from 30 to 60 percent. Many of these were founded by socially conscious entrepreneurs not only to make a profit but also with the aim of protecting the environment and promoting social justice.[8]

Together these new economic institutions are giving communities all over the country a sense of what can be done through collective ownership and management. Their successes and failures provide important lessons for a new, radically decentralized, community-based economy. These new economic institutions are being created not by starry-eyed idealists but out of a need and a void. Their necessity is only heightened by the economic insecurity millions of Americans face in the collapse of the housing bubble, the expansion of layoffs, and the evaporation of personal retirement funds.[9]

Here in Michigan, as in Arizona and elsewhere, we have seen a growing number of average citizens scapegoating blacks, immigrants, and other people of color for their plight. That is why it is becoming increasingly urgent that we consciously try to learn the lessons of the many grassroots efforts to create alternative economic institutions that will not only bring greater stability to our communities but also provide us with the control over the ways in which we make our living that is necessary for a real democracy.

In neighborhoods all over the country, the economic meltdown is forcing people to rethink the waste of suburban living and SUVs and the cost of shopping at malls rather than neighborhood stores. So over holiday dinners amid the crash of 2008, people began swapping stories of an older generation whose hands were more calloused but who cared not only for themselves but for each other. By these diverse means we are embracing the power within us to create the world anew, thereby freeing ourselves from our elected officials in Washington who disempower us by promising solutions that encourage us to think like victims dependent on them for crumbs.

THE NEXT REVOLUTIONARY GENERATION

Over the past forty years I have been blessed with fabulous opportunities to experience the huge changes that have taken place in movement activism since the 1960s. I summed these up in my closing remarks to the tenth annual Allied Media Conference, which met in Detroit in June 2008. This conference draws from all over North America hundreds of diverse participants, many under the age of thirty, who see alternative and noncommercial forms of media as critical means to express nonconformist identities, develop oppositional politics, and strengthen both local and virtual forms of community. The conference organizers, many of whom got started in community-building activism through Detroit Summer, embody the spirit of hope and creativity emanating from Detroit and increasingly rubbing off on the out-of-town participants who come to our city for this annual event.

I felt especially privileged to engage this new generation of movers and shakers. The movements of the sixties, I noted, were led mostly by men coming out of a patriarchal culture. So there was a lot of top-down vertical leadership. At most of our meetings, conferences, and demonstrations, charismatic males made fiery speeches that made bitter and angry masses angrier and more bitter. The focus was on replacing white power with black power. There was a lot of competition for leadership, a lot of militarism.

However, since discovering that the personal is political, women activists have been abandoning the charismatic male, vertical, and vanguard party leadership patterns of the 1960s and creating more participatory, empowering, and horizontal kinds of leadership. Instead of modeling their organizing on the lives of men outside the home—for example, in the plant or in the political arena—they are beginning to model it on the love, caring, healing, and patience that, along with an appreciation of diversity and of strengths and weaknesses, go into the raising of a family.

In the 1960s there was far too little of the love and caring that is an organic part of the everyday lives of women, and no appreciation of the diversity of activities truly necessary to sustain family and community. For example, when women such as Elaine Brown became leaders in those days, it was because they were as tough as men. Ella Baker was a notable exception.

Our meetings, small and large, were mostly meetings to agitate and mobilize faceless masses. There was none of the respectful listening to everyone, no breaking up into small groups so that everyone can participate and contribute, none of the laughter that makes an event like the Allied Media Conference such a joy. Our meetings and our demonstrations lacked the sense that our souls and the souls of those we worked with are growing, that in our relationships and in our community organizing we are patiently building a spiritual framework for our everyday lives. We are not agitating or mobilizing faceless masses but organizing a community base of caring individuals transforming ourselves and becoming the change we want to see in the world.

One of the highlights of the 2008 Allied Media Conference was an especially moving video presented by Sista II Sista, a grassroots community organization based in Brooklyn, New York. These are people in a community, living together like family, taking care of children and of elders, dealing with each other and with conflict in new ways, not out of anger at injustice but from love for one another and for our communities. They are not building power over others but empowering each other. I believe that these and like-minded activists have arrived at these practices mainly because so many activists these days are female and queer.

I was also very moved by Ricardo Dominguez's story of how his group was unwilling to accept that people from Mexico and Central America, struggling to feed themselves and their families in a world where jobs have been eliminated by transnational corporations, are dying by the hundreds as they cross the U.S./ Mexico border because they are not able to tell where they need to go to reach their destination safely or where they can find water. So Electronic Disturbance Theatre, which has pioneered new activist uses of technology to respond to the challenges of the digital age and global economy, is developing cell phones equipped with GPS to provide a virtual geography to mark new trails and potentially safer routes across the desert of the real.

I was particularly impressed with the transparency with which the group is engaging in these lifesaving activities; how they view themselves as acting in the evolutionary humanist tradition of Thoreau, Gandhi, Martin Luther King Jr., the abolitionists, and the Underground Railroad. So they act openly rather than furtively and have thus won respect on both sides of the border.

This, I believe, is the way we need to view our role as American revolutionaries. We are creating a revolutionary alternative to the counterrevolutionary and inhuman policies of the U.S. government, but we are not subversives. We are making the leap forward in the precious human qualities of social responsibility and creativity, now necessary and possible in the evolution of the human species. We are creating the kind of global citizenship that Martin Luther King Jr. said every nation needs to create to preserve the best in its traditions. We are struggling to change this country because we love it.

In Detroit those of us who were in the movements of the sixties arrived at these new practices mainly through our evaluation of those movements, from struggle with the black politicians who came to power after the massive rebellions, from our involvement in the women's movement, and from our involvement with the young people of the Detroit Summer Collective who play a major role in organizing the Allied Media Conference.

I am not dissing or dismissing the black movements and antiwar movements of the 1960s. Without them none of us would be where we are today. The various identity movements—women's; Chicano, Asian American, and Native American; gay and lesbian—were all inspired by both the achievements and the limitations of the sixties. We have all evolved out of these achievements and limitations. That is how each generation develops dialectically from the one that preceded it.

In my eighties and nineties, I have been fortunate to witness the blossoming of new activism all over the place. While my days of marching in demonstrations are well behind me, the struggle to rebuild, redefine, and respirit Detroit from the ground up marches forward: on the west side of town, I see Detroiters establishing centers such as Hush House, where young people and returning prisoners rediscover and rebuild their human identity; on the east side of town, a Hope District helps local residents grow not only food but their souls by weaving new dreams and doing work that serves the needs of the community.

Although my wobbly knees require me to walk with a cane and request wheelchair assistance to move through airports, my travels throughout America have convinced me that our activities in Detroit are part of a wider grassroots movement to transform society. Six years ago, at an Activists and Spirituality Retreat in Kalamazoo, Michigan, I helped create and became a member of the Beloved Communities Initiative (BCI). The initiative grew out of a panel discussion on the last three years of Martin Luther's King Jr.'s life—between myself, Vincent Harding, and John Maguire (both of whom had been close associates of MLK)—and from the new energies that Native American Kathy Sanchez's remarks on the sanctity of water brought to the retreat.

The BCI began with a "These are the times to grow our souls" call to those celebrating MLK's birthday in January 2005 and continued with visits to sites that we identified as in the process of creating new kinds of communities in the United States. These started with Detroit Summer and continued with the annual fall gathering in New Mexico, where Tewa women share the wisdom of indigenous cultures with people of many different backgrounds. Next, we went to Greensboro, North Carolina, where the Beloved Community Center not only has a program and house for the homeless but also has helped create the Truth and Reconciliation Commission as a way for local citizens to grapple with the race and class roots of the KKK massacre of activists during an antiracist march in 1979. The center is now working with youth groups, commonly referred to as gangs, to create peace zones.

We visited Will Allen's urban farm, Growing Power, in Milwaukee, Wisconsin. Will is at the forefront of the urban agricultural movement, which may be the fastest growing movement in the United States. "We're having to go back to when people shared things and started taking care of each other. That's the only way we will survive. What better way than to do it with food?" said Will, as he was honored with a 2008 MacArthur Genius Award.[10]

At Access, the Center for Independent Living in Chicago, we discovered that the prideful struggle of individuals with disabilities is deepening their and our understanding of what it means to be a human being. At Cookman United Methodist Church in North Philadelphia, we spent a weekend with neighborhood residents who had created a loving, caring environment in which young people can complete their schooling and also develop their leadership skills.

We had a great time at a Weaving Faiths retreat with the multiracial performing arts organization Great Leap in South Central Los Angeles, where individuals from a Buddhist temple and a Muslim mosque expanded their identities by doing spiritual and physical rituals and exercises together. In Santa Cruz,

California, "Nane" Alejándrez and other members of Barrios Unidos shared with us their experiences in working with present inmates and ex-prisoners to create restorative rather than punitive justice. Our visit to the Poverty Initiative at the Union Theological Seminary in New York provided an opportunity to meet local groups created by the poor to end poverty.

These visits have reaffirmed my belief that the movement today, in this period and this country, is being created not by the cadres of a vanguard party with a common ideology, but by individuals and groups responding creatively with passion and imagination to the real problems and challenges that they face where they live and work.

In earlier chapters I have already named just a few of these individuals whom I have met. I am sure that there are many, many more whom you know and whom I have not met.

They/we are the leaders we are looking for.

NOTES

INTRODUCTION BY SCOTT KURASHIGE

1. Grace Lee Boggs, *Living for Change: An Autobiography* (Minneapolis: University of Minnesota Press, 1998), 149.

2. Stating his pressing need to travel abroad and develop a new organization of his own, Malcolm declined. See Grace Lee Boggs, *Living for Change,* 133–36.

3. For instance, historian Stephen Ward has found records of a U.S. Senate committee hearing in which William R. McCoy, a detective lieutenant from the Detroit Police Department, remarks about Grace, "I believe she is of Chinese and African descent." McCoy wrongly identifies her as Grace Lillian Boggs ("a housewife") and lists an incorrect birth date and PhD graduation date. See U.S. Senate, *Riots, Civil and Criminal Disorders: Hearings before the Permanent Subcommittee on Investigations of the Committee on Government Operations,* pt. 6, 90th Cong., 2nd sess., March 21–22 (Washington: U.S. Government Printing Office, 1968), 1439–40.

4. For an introduction to Detroit history, see Thomas Sugrue, *The Origins of the Urban Crisis: Race and Inequality in Postwar Detroit* (Princeton, NJ: Princeton University Press, 2005).

5. *Detroit News,* August 8, 1967.

6. Rebecca Solnit, "Detroit Arcadia: Exploring the Post-American Landscape," *Harper's Magazine*, July 2007, 73.

7. Alex Altman, "Detroit Tries to Get on a Road to Renewal," *Time*, April 6, 2009, 40–45; John Huey, "Why Time Inc. Is in Motown," *Time*, October 5, 2009, 4.

8. John Reed, "The Travails of Detroit," *Financial Times*, March 6, 2009.

9. Jerry Herron, *Afterculture: Detroit and the Humiliation of History* (Detroit, MI: Wayne State University Press, 1993), 9.

10. Immanuel Wallerstein, *The Decline of American Power* (New York: New Press, 2003).

CHAPTER 1. THESE ARE THE TIMES TO GROW OUR SOULS

Animating Democracy, a program of Americans for the Arts, commissioned Grace to serve as the featured presenter for the National Exchange on Art and Civic Dialogue in 2003. Her talk, which served as an earlier and shorter version of this chapter, subsequently appeared on its Web site as an article titled "These Are the Times That Try Our Souls."

1. This series of questions is similar to those posed in the article by Grace Lee Boggs, "Thinking Dialectically toward Community," in *Pedagogies of the Global: Knowledge in the Human Interest*, ed. Arif Dirlik (Boulder, CO: Paradigm, 2006), 299–300.

2. See Martin Luther King Jr., "A Time to Break Silence," in *A Testament of Hope: The Essential Writings and Speeches of Martin Luther King, Jr.*, ed. James M. Washington (New York: Harper Collins, 1991), 231–44.

3. Daniel Schorr, *Come to Think of It: Notes on the End of the Millennium* (New York: Viking Penguin, 2007), 208; Jack Lessenberry, "Crimes Low and High," *MetroTimes*, December 13, 2000.

4. Starhawk, "Only Poetry Can Address Grief: Moving Forward after 911," *Starhawk's Tangled Web*, www.starhawk.org/activism/activism-writings/movingforward.html.

5. Alice Calaprice, ed. *The New Quotable Einstein* (Princeton, NJ: Princeton University Press, 2005), 9, 175.

6. *New York Times,* March 29, 1972.

7. Rosemarie Freeney Harding and Rachel E. Harding, "Radical Hospitality: How Kitchen-Table Lessons in Welcome and Respect Helped Sustain the Black Freedom Movement," *Sojourners Magazine,* July–August 2003, 42–46.

8. Rachel Carson, *Silent Spring* (Boston: Houghton Mifflin, 1962), 2.

9. Paul Hawken, *Blessed Unrest: How the Largest Movement in the World Came into Being and Why No One Saw It Coming* (New York: Viking, 2007).

10. Joanna Macy, "The Great Turning as Compass and Lens," *YES!* Summer 2006, www.yesmagazine.org/issues/5000-years-of-empire/the-great-turning-as-compass-and-lens.

11. Karen Armstrong, *The Great Transformation: The Beginning of Our Religious Traditions* (New York: Knopf, 2006).

12. King, "Time to Break Silence," 242.

13. I am reminded of Che Guevara's oft-cited comment: "At the risk of seeming ridiculous, let me say that a true revolutionary is guided by great feelings of love." As Mitchel Cohen further notes, "Che called upon radicals to transform OURSELVES into new, socialist human beings BEFORE the revolution, if we were to have any hope of actually achieving one worth living in." See "Revolution Guided by Feelings of Great Love: Learning from Che Guevara," *CounterPunch,* January 3–4, 2004, www.counterpunch.org/cohen01032004.html.

Exploring King's concept can help us understand why Che's statement has been so puzzling to traditional radicals and why Che lives on in the hearts of young revolutionaries. For example, theologians and lawyers Barbara A. Holmes and Susan Holmes Winfield challenge us to think more expansively about King's concept of Love as *a foundational principle for social change:*

"When we are confronted by the infrastructures of malignant social systems," they write, "love seems frail at best and irrelevant at worst. Yet, the lessons of history teach just the opposite. In defiance of our logic, love has sustained whole communities. With nothing more than love, besieged people confront radical evil, endure losses, bury their dead, and console each other during and after the devastation."

"For King, love is synonymous with ethics," Holmes and Winfield argue. "It is a moral principle that provides context, norms, rules of engagement, and a vision of moral flourishing." They conclude, "The strength of King's belief in the law, his abiding faith in love as praxis, and the force of his performative acts forged crosscultural alliances and inspired even the courts to interpret the laws in a manner that for a time changed the face of the nation. . . . Using love's untapped potential, he awakened a nation to its shortcomings and African Americans to the fullness of their humanity."

See "King, the Constitution, and the Courts," in *The Legacy of Martin Luther King, Jr.: The Boundaries of Law, Politics, and Religion,* ed. Lewis V. Baldwin, with Rufus Burrow Jr., Barbara A. Holmes, and Susan Holmes Winfield (Notre Dame, IN: University of Notre Dame Press, 2002), 173–211.

14. Margaret Wheatley, *Leadership and the New Science: Discovering Order in a Chaotic World* (San Francisco: Berrett-Koehler, 1999), 44–45.

CHAPTER 2. REVOLUTION AS
A NEW BEGINNING

The title of this chapter, along with some snippets of text, is drawn from Adrian Harewood and Tom Keefer, "Revolution as a New Beginning: An Interview with Grace Lee Boggs," *Upping the Anti: A Journal of Theory and Action,* no. 1 (2005): 15–30, no. 2 (2006): 36–47.

1. Immanuel Wallerstein, *The Modern World-System: Capitalist Agriculture and the Origins of the European World-Economy in the Sixteenth Century* (New York: Academic Press, 1974); Gertrud Lenzer, "Searching for the Present in the Past," review of *The Modern World-System,* by Immanuel Wallerstein, *New York Times,* December 29, 1974.

2. Wallerstein, *After Liberalism* (New York: New Press, 1995).

3. Wallerstein, *Utopistics; or, Historical Choices of the Twenty-First Century* (New York: New Press, 1998), 31–32.

4. Wallerstein, *The End of the World as We Know It: Social Science for the Twenty-First Century* (Minneapolis: University of Minnesota Press, 1999).

5. For a deeper discussion of the autobiographical issues addressed in this chapter, see Grace Lee Boggs, *Living for Change*, esp. chs. 2–6.

6. In 1939 I decided to write my dissertation on "George Herbert Mead: The Philosopher of the Social Individual" because I needed to move beyond the university and create myself as a social individual, and he provided me with a philosophy that stated, "It is through interaction with other individuals that the self is created." For the published version of this dissertation, see Grace Chin Lee, *George Herbert Mead: The Philosopher of the Social Individual* (New York: King's Crown, 1945).

As an American philosopher who had studied in Germany and was a student of European philosophy (which was the only topic that courses in philosophy at U.S. universities taught in that period), Mead also understood that Americans are profoundly different from Europeans. We Americans are conscious of our founding in a way that other peoples are not. Also, we can never evade the fact that contradictions were built into our founding. Therefore, we are constantly in the process of creating and re-creating ourselves. We can't believe, as Hobbes did, that the self is only selfish—or like Locke, that the self is naturally social. By hook or by crook, we are constantly challenged to believe, as Rousseau did, to act on the conviction that through communicating or covenanting with others, we can become both subject and sovereign; or as Kant did, that just as our minds give form to reality, we can re-create reality by acting as if our actions could become a universal law.

Mead was born in 1863, around the same time as John Dewey (1859) and Jane Addams (1860). Members of his generation, the generation of civic passions, gave birth to social democracy because they refused to accept a dichotomy between the True and the Good. In my twilight years I increasingly realize how lucky I am that I was introduced in my early twenties to social democracy in the person of Mead, then to

Marxist-Leninism by way of C. L. R. James, and then to (r)evolution with Jimmy Boggs.

7. C. L. R. James, *The Black Jacobins: Toussaint l'Ouverture and the San Domingo Revolution* (New York: Dial, 1939).

8. Grace translated three of these early essays by Marx from German into English for a publication, which the Johnson-Forest Tendency introduced as the first English translations of his *Economic and Philosophic Manuscripts* of 1843–44. See *Essays by Karl Marx, Selected from the Economic and Philosophic Manuscripts* (New York: Johnson-Forest Tendency, 1947).

9. Karl Marx and Friedrich Engels, *Manifesto of the Communist Party,* in *The Marx-Engels Reader,* ed. Robert C. Tucker (New York: Norton, 1978), 476.

10. Georg Wilhelm Friedrich Hegel, *The Phenomenology of Mind,* trans. J. B. Baillie (New York: Macmillan, 1931), 81.

11. Marx, "The Civil War in France," in *The Paris Commune,* ed. Lucien Sanial (New York: New York Labor News, 1902), 78.

12. Marx, *Capital: A Critique of Political Economy* (New York: Kerr, 1906), 836–37.

13. James Boggs, *The American Revolution: Pages from a Negro Worker's Notebook* (New York: Monthly Review, 1963), 83. In 2009 Monthly Review Press reissued this book with a new introduction by Grace Lee Boggs and commentaries by Shea Howell, Carl Edwards, Larry Sparks, Julia Pointer-Putnam, Jeanette Lee, and Rich Feldman.

14. James and Grace Lee Boggs, *Revolution and Evolution in the Twentieth Century* (New York: Monthly Review, 1974), 16–17.

15. Ibid., 140.

16. See Vincent Harding, *Martin Luther King: An Inconvenient Hero,* rev. ed. (Maryknoll, NY: Orbis Books, 2008).

17. For more about the Zapatistas, see El Kilombo Intergalactico, *Beyond Resistance: Everything, an Interview with Subcomandante Marcos* (Durham, NC: PaperBoat, 2007).

18. Thomas S. Kuhn, *The Structure of Scientific Revolutions* (Chicago: University of Chicago Press, 1962).

CHAPTER 3. LET'S TALK ABOUT MALCOLM
AND MARTIN

Portions of this chapter appeared in earlier form in the new introduction by Grace Lee Boggs to the reissue of James and Grace Lee Boggs, *Revolution and Evolution in the Twentieth Century* (New York: Monthly Review, 2008), xxii–xvi.

1. Jan Carew, *Ghosts in Our Blood: With Malcolm X in Africa, England, and the Caribbean* (New York: Lawrence Hill Books, 1994), 36.

2. Vincent Harding wrote the first draft of MLK's April 4, 1967, historic anti–Vietnam War speech, "A Time to Break Silence." Years later, he discussed his role in writing King's speech and expanded the ideas in the 1984 pamphlet, *A Way of Faith, a Time for Courage*. See *Martin Luther King: The Inconvenient Hero*, rev. ed. (Maryknoll, NY: Orbis Books, 2008).

3. For example, *We Shall Overcome: Martin Luther King Jr. and the Black Freedom Movement*, ed. Peter J. Albert and Ronald Hoffman (New York: DaCapo, 1993), is a compilation of papers presented by an impressive group of scholars and activists.

4. See Grace Lee Boggs, "Thoughts on the Black Radical Congress," *Michigan Citizen*, May 10, 1998.

5. Hegel, *Phenomenology of Mind*, 10.

6. See Mahatma Gandhi, *Selected Political Writings*, ed. Dennis Dalton (Indianapolis: Hackett, 1996), 7.

7. Martin Luther King Jr., *Where Do We Go from Here: Community or Chaos?* (New York: Harper and Row, 1967), 156. These quotes from King, as well as additional quotes and paraphrased readings of his works that follow in this chapter, were previously incorporated into Grace Lee Boggs, "Thinking Dialectically toward Community," 301–5.

8. King, *Where Do We Go*, 171–72, 185–86.

9. Ibid., 187.

10. Ibid., 163–64.

11. King, "Time to Break Silence," 231–44.

12. Ibid. On page 241, King expands on the concept of a revolution of values:

A true revolution of values will soon look uneasily on the glaring contrast of poverty and wealth. With righteous indignation, it will look across the seas and see individual capitalists of the West investing huge sums of money in Asia, Africa and South America, only to take the profits out with no concern for the social betterment of the countries, and say: "This is not just." The Western arrogance of feeling that it has everything to teach others and nothing to learn from them is not just. A true revolution of values will lay hands on the world order and say of war: "This way of settling differences is not just." This business of burning human beings with napalm, of filling our nation's homes with orphans and widows, of injecting poisonous drugs of hate into the veins of peoples normally humane, of sending men home from dark and bloody battlefields physically handicapped and psychologically deranged, cannot be reconciled with wisdom, justice and love. A nation that continues year after year to spend more money on military defense than on programs of social uplift is approaching spiritual death.

13. King, *Trumpet of Conscience,* in *Testament of Hope,* 641, 644.

14. Ibid., 643, 645, 651.

15. King, "Our Struggle," in *Testament of Hope,* 76.

16. Yusef Shakur, *The Window 2 My Soul: My Transformation from a Zone 8 Thug to a Father & Freedom Fighter* (Detroit: Urban Guerrilla Entertainment, 2008). To order this book, go to www.yusefshakur.org/.

17. "Demands of the Detroit Coalition against Police Brutality," www.detroitcoalition.org/about.

CHAPTER 4. DETROIT, PLACE AND SPACE
TO BEGIN ANEW

Portions of this chapter appeared in earlier form in the new introduction by Grace Lee Boggs to the 2008 reissue of Boggs, *Revolution and Evolution,* xviii–xxii.

1. Sugrue, *Urban Crisis,* 259.

2. David Fastenfast, "Community Politics and Urban Redevelopment: Poletown, Detroit, and General Motors," *Urban Affairs Review* 22 (September 1986): 101–23.

3. Grace Lee Boggs, *Living for Change,* 218.

4. Ibid.

5. James Boggs, "Black Power: A Scientific Concept Whose Time Has Come," in *Racism and the Class Struggle: Further Pages from a Black Worker's Notebook* (New York: Monthly Review, 1970), 60.

6. Grace Lee Boggs, *Living for Change*, 231–32.

7. For more on ICUE, see Kyong Park, ed., *Urban Ecology: Detroit and Beyond* (Hong Kong: Map Book, 2005).

8. Curt Guyette, "Down a Green Path," *MetroTimes*, October 31, 2001.

9. Grace Lee Boggs, "Detroiters Point Way for Twenty-First-Century Cities," *Michigan Citizen*, November 25, 2007.

10. Solnit, "Detroit Arcadia," 73.

11. Michele Owens, "The Emerald City," *O Magazine*, April 2008, 256–59, 274 (quote on 274).

12. Michael Hardt and Antonio Negri, *Multitude: War and Democracy in the Age of Empire* (New York: Penguin, 2004).

13. Maria Mies and Veronika Bennholdt-Thomsen, *The Subsistence Perspective: Beyond the Globalized Economy* (London: Zed Books, 2000); Mies and Vandana Shiva, *Ecofeminism* (London: Zed Books, 1993).

CHAPTER 5. A PARADIGM SHIFT IN OUR CONCEPT OF EDUCATION

1. Grace Lee Boggs, "Education: The Great Obsession," in *Education and Black Struggle: Notes from the Colonized World*, ed. Institute of the Black World (Cambridge, MA: Harvard Educational Review, 1974), 61–81.

2. Alvin Toffler, *The Third Wave* (New York: Morrow, 1980).

3. Renate Nummela Caine and Geoffrey Caine, *Making Connections: Teaching and the Human Brain* (Alexandria, VA: Association for Supervision and Curriculum Development, 1991), and *Education on the Edge of Possibility* (Alexandria, VA: Association for Supervision and Curriculum Development, 1997).

4. Martin S. Dworkin, ed., *Dewey on Education* (New York: Teachers College, 1959), 39–40.

5. Ibid., 22, 47.

6. Ibid., 50–51, 76–78.

7. Richard L. Johnson, ed., *Gandhi's Experiments with Truth* (Lanham, MD: Lexington Books, 2005), 111–12.

8. Paulo Freire, *Cultural Action for Freedom* (Cambridge, MA: Harvard Educational Review, 2000), 50, 56.

9. Boggs, *Revolution and Evolution* (1974), 17–19.

10. Paulo Freire, *Pedagogy of the Oppressed* (New York: Herder and Herder, 1970).

11. Neil Postman and Charles Weingartner, *Teaching as a Subversive Activity* (New York: Delacorte, 1969).

12. Sigmund Freud, *Civilization and Its Discontents*, trans. and ed. James Strachey (New York: Norton, 1989); John Dewey, *The School and Society* (Chicago: University of Chicago Press, 1899).

13. Postman, *The Disappearance of Childhood* (New York: Delacorte, 1982), esp. 77–119.

14. George Siemens writes with a focus on education and learning in the digital age. Most of his writing is distributed digitally on the Internet. See his Web site at www.elearnspace.org/.

CHAPTER 6. WE ARE THE LEADERS WE'VE BEEN LOOKING FOR

1. Gwendolyn Zoharah Simmons, "Following the Call," Veterans of Hope Pamphlet Series 1, No. 4 (Denver: A Center for the Study of Religion and Democratic Renewal, 2000), 12.

2. Rob "Biko" Baker, "Last Night I Waved an American Flag," August 29, 2008, http://theleague.com/last-night/. Special thanks to Biko for permitting the authors to reprint significant portions of this Web posting.

3. For the complete transcript of this discussion, see *Democracy Now!* "Novelist Alice Walker and Activist Grace Lee Boggs React to Obama's Inauguration," January 21, 2009, www.democracynow.org/2009/1/21/novelist_alice_walker_and_activist_grace.

4. Grace Lee Boggs, "What Do We Do Now?" *Michigan Citizen*, February 1, 2009.

5. Vincent Harding, "Midwifing a New America," *OneLife Institute News* (Autumn 2008): 3–4.

6. See the complete "Principles of Environmental Justice" adopted in October 1991, www.ejnet.org/ej/principles.html.

7. Ethan Miller, "Independence from the Corporate Global Economy," *YES!* Winter 2007, www.yesmagazine.org/article.asp?ID=1545.

8. Gar Alperovitz, *America beyond Capitalism: Reclaiming Our Wealth, Our Liberty and Our Democracy* (Hoboken, NJ: Wiley, 2004).

9. Information on new economic institutions' locations and advice on how to organize and learn from their experiences can be found on the Web site of the Democracy Collaborative, www.community-wealth.org/.

10. *New York Times*, October 1, 2008.

AFTERWORD: IN CONVERSATION WITH
IMMANUEL WALLERSTEIN

*One of the most electrifying and well-attended events of the second United States Social
Forum was a conversation between Grace Lee Boggs and Immanuel Wallerstein. The
following is an edited transcript of that historic conversation, held before a standing-
room-only crowd of seven hundred people on June 24, 2010 in Detroit's Cobo Center.*

*In this animated dialogue about the past, present, and future of social transforma-
tion, Grace's rootedness in Detroit, with its largely working-class African American
population and its localized response to industrial collapse, is perfectly complemented by
Wallerstein's command of the global sweep of history and political economy spanning
multiple centuries and continents. Scott Kurashige served as moderator.*

SK: I am deeply honored to moderate this historic conversation
between two movement elders—two paradigmatic figures who
collectively embody well over one hundred years of political
engagement: Grace Lee Boggs and Immanuel Wallerstein.

GLB: Thank you all for coming, and thank you, Immanuel, for
coming to Detroit.

Since I first met Immanuel Wallerstein on the first page
of the *New York Times Book Review* in 1975, I've read him and
I've quoted him over and over again. He helps us to see that
we can very easily get trapped in the ideas of the past while
reality is constantly changing. In his wonderful book called

Utopistics he writes that, after 1968, the ideas we had been living by since the French Revolution had become outmoded. And in a paragraph that I use all the time, he says, "The world of 2050 will be what we make it."

There are very few times in history where the free will factor matters as much as it does today. All of us, each of us, must live by that conception: that the world of 2050 will be what we make it; that we have the power within us to change the world. And that's the role that intellectuals can play. Many of you are intellectuals. Many of you are college students. And when you join a revolutionary or radical organization, you're likely to believe that only practice matters, that only action matters, and you become mindless activists living by old ideas. I hope our conversation today will provide you with an opportunity to understand what it means to create new ideas as reality changes.

IW: I'm terribly delighted to be here and to be with Grace Boggs. Grace Boggs is someone I've known and admired for a long time because she incarnates for me the idea that though the struggle is long, the struggle is also immediate—that everybody lives in the present as well as in the future, and you have to take care of the present if you're going to have any realistic impact on the future. So she's tried to combine working always in the present here in Detroit at the local level—to do things that will make life better immediately for people who are here—and also to try to transform the world in a longer-range prospect. So that's what we're going to talk about today—how to do that.

SK: We're going to start with our panelists giving us their sense of how they see the world today. What are the core concepts that we need to make sense of the challenges we confront?

GLB: I had the great privilege of coming to Detroit in 1953, when the Japanese were not yet producing cars. We were still the Motor City, motor capital of the world. So I have lived through Detroit being the national and international symbol of

the miracles of industrialization to it becoming a nat
international symbol of the devastation of deindustr
And today you've come to Detroit because it's becoming the
national and international symbol of a new kind of society—a
society where the gulf between the industrial and the agrar-
ian epoch is becoming resolved. Not because anyone thought
that would be desirable, but because living at the expense
of the earth and living at the expense of other peoples have
brought us to the edge of disaster. So it's up to us. It's that
time on the clock of the universe where we face our evolution
to a higher humanity or the devastation and the extinction of
all life on earth. It's a fantastic period. You've probably seen
these T-shirts from the Boggs Center that say "evolution." To
understand that revolution is also evolution is what I have
learned from my years of practice.

IW: The way I approach this is to say we all live, everybody lives,
in historical systems, and historical systems do not go on
forever. We're living in one that we call "capitalism" or the
"capitalist world-economy" or the "modern world-system." It
came into existence about five hundred years ago.

You have to explain how it came into existence, but we're
not going to talk about that today. Then it goes on. It has a
normal life, and you can understand that normal life. You
can analyze it. I've been trying to do that; other people have
been trying to do that for a long time. But systems don't go on
forever. They move slowly, slowly away from equilibrium until
they get too far away. And that's in fact where the modern
world-system is today.

The modern world-system has entered into its structural
crisis. It's coming to an end. It's not coming to an end just
because lots of people are oppressed and don't like it. That's
been true for a very, very long time. That's not what's new.
What's new is that the system doesn't provide the possibilities
in its own terms to work. "Its own terms" is an endless
accumulation of capital. It's kind of a crazy system. You run, in
order to run, in order to run, in order to run. And it's worked

brilliantly. It worked very well for a couple of hundred years, but it has moved far away from equilibrium and gotten into what we call a structural crisis. When you're in a structural crisis, the alternatives are not only for you who are oppressed or we who are oppressed but for the people who oppress us. They too see that the system is coming to an end. They too have to worry about what comes next. And that's the long-term struggle that we're in today. It's a struggle in which there are two fundamental sides—not about preserving the present system but about what will replace it. We're in the middle of that.

Grace talked about the "free will factor." What happens when the system goes on normally, which it did for several hundred years, is that there's a very strong pressure to come back to equilibrium, so that no matter how far you push it from equilibrium, the pressures push it back. That's what happened to the French Revolution; that's what happened to the Russian Revolution. There was an enormous amount of social action and social pressure to create something new, but after a while the system pushed it back. That's what we usually call "determinism."

But when a system gets so far from equilibrium that it just doesn't work anymore, there's nothing that can push it back to equilibrium. That's when the so-called free will factor comes in. That's when every little action on our part helps to determine the end—the end that we don't know. That's really terribly important to underline: *We don't know who's going to win the struggle of the next twenty to fifty years, to define what system will replace the present system.*

We don't know. We may win. We may not win. There's no certainty on that. But it all depends on us because who wins is a matter of the addition of everybody's effort at every moment in every part of the world.

And the other side has a lot going for it. They've got money, they've got guns, they've got intelligence, they've got power. All right? So they are not going to give up easily. All right? But that doesn't mean they can't be beaten. And that's where we are. We're in the middle of a big struggle about how to replace the present awful system in which we live with one that is better. That's why we say, "Another world is possible." I underline the word *possible.* It's possible. It's not certain; it's possible. That's what's up to us.

GLB: It's so important to understand the difference between *possible* and *necessary.* When I became a radical many years ago, I wanted certainty, I wanted necessity, and I embraced Marxism for that reason. And I'm not an anti-Marxist, but I think we need to look at ourselves and understand what we're talking about is uncertainty—that revolution is a new beginning. It's not to prove that our analysis is correct, although many radicals think that's what it's about.

At the end of his book on *The End Of The World As We Know It,* which I recommend, Immanuel says that in uncertainty there is hope. That is such a fundamental concept to understand. I don't know how many of you know other languages. But fortunately I've studied German. So I look at words more critically. I feel the huge difference between the possible and the necessary. So I know that there is much more hope, much more need for us to make choices in the possible than in the necessary. That *möglichkeit* is more important than *notwendigkeit.* My German is very bad.

IW: That was very good.

GLB: When you read Immanuel's writing on the modern world-system, which is not easy reading, you'll see that the feudal system came to an end because they could no longer cope with the new realities. That will help you understand what's happening in the Gulf of Mexico [with the Deepwater Horizon oil spill], in the White House, and to the shareholders of BP in a way that you will not get just from looking at TV. There's a way in which history, philosophy, and theory help you understand reality at a much deeper level. I hope that's what you'll get out of this conversation.

sk: So we want to understand why the system is in crisis today.
What are the key aspects of that crisis and what are the key
openings and challenges moving toward the future? But first,
I want to ask our panelists to concretize what we mean when
we talk about this "system." People are here at the U.S. Social
Forum because they know there is something terribly wrong
with this system, that there are deep problems with greed and
injustice and oppression. But capitalism is not the first system
to be rooted in greed and injustice and oppression. What is
specific about capitalism that we need to understand if we're
to make sense of what the system represents and what we must
do to transcend it?

iw: Well, capitalism is a system that is based on the idea that
there should be an endless accumulation of capital. You
accumulate capital, in order to accumulate capital, in order
to accumulate capital, in order to accumulate capital. You're
on this treadmill, or what they call the things that rats run on.
OK? And it depends on something called "growth." You notice
people talking about growth all the time, and they say we have
to do this, we have to do that in order to ensure growth.

Now growth per se is not a plus or a minus. Cancer is
growth too. So these days in the indigenous movements
of the Americas, they talk a lot about—it's hard to say it
in English; in various languages they have terms. It gets
translated into Spanish as *buen vivir*: "to live well." To live well
is not necessarily to endlessly consume. It is indeed to make
some sort of rational arrangement with the world with the
possibility of fulfilling oneself individually and collectively—
and that requires restraints as well as growth. So that's the kind
of system that hopefully we want to create.

Now this isn't the kind of system that the people at Davos
want to create. They want to create another kind of system.
It doesn't have to be capitalism; it won't be capitalism. It will
be something else. It could be much worse than capitalism.
Capitalism isn't necessarily the worst possible system in the
world. You can invent worse ones.

The capitalist system has the consequence of exploitation, of hierarchy, and of polarization. There's been enormous polarization over the past five hundred years and particularly in the past fifty years. It's been incredible—the degree of polarization, the gap between those, not even just the 1 percent, the 20 percent who do reasonably well in the world and the 80 percent who don't do reasonably well in the world. Now that's the kind of system we have at the moment.

They're trying to find another kind of system that will do that. I don't know the name of that system. They don't know the name of that system. They'll try to invent it. We've got to try to invent a different one.

But we've got to talk about the consequences of this for organizing. People live in the present. Everybody has to eat today, not tomorrow. Everybody has to sleep today, not tomorrow. Everybody has to do all those ordinary things today, and you can't tell people that they have to just wait another five or ten or twenty years, and it's going to get better somehow. Indeed that was a line of a lot of the historic antisystemic movements: "It will be better tomorrow; the sunshine is beyond the horizon." So you've got to worry about today, but you can't *only* worry about today.

The problem is working out a strategy that combines a very short-run, immediate attempt to solve people's needs and a medium-run strategy of transforming the system. I think of the very short run as one of minimizing the pain. Minimizing the pain can be done in a thousand different ways. Some of it requires government action. Some of it requires popular action. But people need to have less pain immediately, and there are all sorts of ways of doing that. That doesn't transform the world, but it does meet people's needs.

But you've also got to explain to people, explain to yourself, that we've got a twenty- to thirty- to forty-year struggle here. Now we have to think about the things that will win this struggle over the next twenty, thirty, forty, fifty years—to come out of the chaotic situation we are in now, the highly

fluctuating situation that we are in now, into a new *better* order
rather than a new *worse* order. There will be some new system
emerging, and at some point it will crystallize.

GLB: I think it's so important to think about the word "system."
Years ago when I became a radical—some of you young
people have become radicals in the last period—I thought
of the system as a thing, something you could erase off the
blackboard like a thing that was intact. I didn't realize that the
capitalist system was a concept people had created because,
living in a situation of scarcity, economic growth seemed very
necessary to them.

I want you to think about this: "How do you as
theoreticians, as intellectuals, and as activists think about
change in a very personal way?"

For example, in the 1970s and 1980s, all we could see in
Detroit were vacant lots, abandoned houses, rot, and blight.
But some African American women, particularly elders raised
in the South, saw these vacant lots as places where you could
grow food to meet a basic need. And they didn't think of basic
needs only in terms of belly hunger. They thought of the need
for urban kids to grow up with a sense of process, to have a
sense of how it takes time for things to happen, for change
to occur. They thought of urban agriculture as a means for
cultural change in young people.

The urban agricultural movement developed out of that
reality, out of the very human needs of real people. And that's
why it's so important that the second U.S. Social Forum is
meeting in Detroit.

IW: One of the fundamental aspects of capitalism as a system is
what I call the commodification of everything. You want to
turn all activities into activities which are done for a profit in
order that there be growth and capital accumulation. Actually
commodification hasn't been all that easy for capitalism. Up
to about fifty years ago there were lots of things that weren't

commodified. Water by and large was not commodified, hospitals weren't commodified . . .

GB: Sex wasn't commodified!

IW: You jumped. I wanted to go in between that. Universities weren't commodified, and yes, sex wasn't commodified. Well, certain kinds of sex were commodified, but other kinds were not. And the body wasn't commodified. But in the last thirty to fifty years we've seen this mad rush to commodify more and more and more of these things in order to find a last bit of growth in these areas as others dry up.

Now one of the things we can do in the short run is to try to *de*commodify—in part to stop this thrust toward madness but also to test the alternative possibilities of what will work in a more decommodified world. We don't really know how it all could work. We've got to experiment, and that's something we can all do in the short run as part of the process of trying to make the transition from where we are now into this other world which is possible.

GLB: And we are not alone. The resistance to commodification is a human resistance. It's not something that comes out of a book or out of theory. All over the world, along with corporate globalization, we have resistance developing. People are resisting the commodification of all our relationships. They're resisting the commodification of our environment, of our communities, and that's why you're here. We are creating a new movement for rehumanization, for a radical revolution of values.

I don't know how many of you read Martin Luther King's speech against the Vietnam war. We need to understand that what he is talking about is how we have been dehumanized by materialism, we have been dehumanized by militarism, we have been dehumanized by consumerism. To understand the extent to which that has happened since World War II is something we really need to do, so that we don't talk about systems in the abstract. We need to know how we have become part of the system and how the movement that we're engaged in is for not only the transformation of institutions but the transformation of ourselves

SK: OK, so this is really a key point we need to emphasize: that the purpose of this system is to put a price tag on every resource, every human action, even on every thought and feeling and emotion. It wants to commodify everything. And I think what Grace is really emphasizing is that what you can see in places like Detroit is not just people growing gardens to feed themselves and to give them the healthy produce that's very difficult to find in inner-city neighborhoods. You see people doing this in order to resist this form of relationship that says "everything must be bought and sold, and everything must be done for the sake of a capitalist profit."

I want to switch gears now and talk about the current moment that we're in. Obviously there's been a huge financial meltdown, a recession. The United States is still quagmired in Iraq, and we see in the headlines today how badly things are going in Afghanistan. But this is not the first recession or depression; this is not the first war gone awry. What is unique about this moment, when did this crisis begin, and how can we really understand what this crisis represents so that we can prepare ourselves to struggle to change the world?

IW: Well, gee, the crisis is bigger. First of all it's not a recession; we're in a *depression*. People don't want to use the word, as though not using the word will wash it away.

We're in a situation where the choices are impossible because the fluctuations of the world market are so radical that it's impossible in a very short run to predict. People sit around with piles of money, for example, in pension funds—lots of you have money in pension funds—and they have to make decisions where to invest. What's been happening is that the money possibilities have been going up and down so fast that they've been losing money, making money, losing money, and they're not sure whether they should put their money into dollars or yen or Euros or something else. So of course they make mistakes. And the governments say, "what can we do about it?"

Well, you know what they do about it. What they do is that they cut the pension funds. So that increases the pain enormously, but it doesn't solve the problem at all. And the degree of fluctuation is so hard that people can't make short-run rational decisions. When they can't make short-run rational decisions, they panic. Individuals panic, capitalists panic, all sorts of people panic.

If you want to understand right-wing populism in the United States—or, indeed, in Europe or in other parts of the world today—understand it in terms of people panicking. They don't know how to protect themselves. They do see that they're in a shaky situation, and they lash out at whatever. That leads to xenophobia: You find the enemy and attack it in a way that doesn't solve any of your problems, but it makes you feel better for a few minutes—until the next time that it doesn't work.

That also explains electoral fluctuations, which have been tremendous in the last few years. Everybody knows Spain is in trouble, right? It's got too much debt and so forth and so on. And everybody's been telling Spain, the government, that what you've got to do is cut down your expenses, cut your budgets, and so forth. The Spanish parliament voted the severest cuts in the history of Spain. The very next day the Fitch ratings downgraded Spain's bonds. And the argument—they gave it in writing—was that cutting the budget reduces the possibility of growth, which it does.

But there it is: Damned if you do, damned if you don't. If you *don't* do it, you're damned because you're a spendthrift and allowing the budget to get out of hand. And if you *do* do it, you're cutting the possibility of growth. Well, what do you do if you're a government? There isn't any good thing to do, and that's what virtually all the governments of the world today are facing. They don't have a good choice. Whatever they choose, it's damned if you do and damned if you don't. It's a losing game, and voters blame them. Well, they've got to blame somebody, and they blame the government in power. And they vote somebody else into power, who does what? They're faced with the same impossible choices. That's the present situation in the world.

SK: So one of the very important points we take away from Professor Wallerstein is the idea that liberal reform was done not just because there were some bleeding heart do-gooders who wanted to help people. These reforms were designed to stabilize the capitalist system and also to make people believe that the system worked—and if it wasn't working, that it could be fixed. And that's why it's so much in crisis, because those liberal reforms can't work. It's a "damned if you do, damned if you don't" situation.

Grace, I want you to talk about what you from your perspective see as the key aspects of the crisis of this system and what you want people to take away from this moment.

GLB: Well, first of all, I think we need to understand why the World Social Forum began in the first place. It began after the Battle of Seattle. You remember when fifty thousand people came out—Teamsters, [United] Steelworkers, women, young people—and they shut down the WTO [World Trade Organization]. Within a couple of years the World Social Forum began at Porto Alegre, announcing "Another world is necessary, another world is possible." But participants weren't quite clear about where this other world was happening.

That's why I want folks to read the commentaries that Wallerstein puts out every couple of weeks. Because they help you understand that it [the failure of U.S. foreign policy] is not only about Obama being weak; he may be. It's not only about [General David] Petraeus being ambitious; he may be. It's about how the whole thing has become dysfunctional. And what do you do when something has become dysfunctional? Do you keep demonstrating and hoping that it becomes more functional? Or do you begin projecting and creating alternatives? And where do you look for these alternatives? You look for these alternatives among ordinary people who are trying to satisfy very basic human needs—needs for food, the need to know where you are in the world, the need to reassert your human identity.

I believe we think of the movements of the Sixties too much in terms of particular identities—as the identities of blacks or Latinos or Asian Americans or women. They should all be seen as part of a search for a new human identity, and we're still engaged in that search.

When you think that way—when you understand why movements are created, why new worlds are created, and why new systems are created—that shapes what you do with your time and how you organize. It's not just something that you understand because you're born, you're human, and you know everything. You have to be able to think philosophically and historically.

I emphasize that because so many of you here are young people who are in university and are trying to figure out "what should you do with your mind?" Does your mind have a role in movement activism? Is it important to think and not just act? This is the time not only to act but to think—to understand that philosophy is not only an abstraction, but that it is also a way of thinking about thinking. We can think with our hearts, or we can think only with the left side of our brains. And we're learning so much from neuroscience now about how our brains are much more complex and how knowledge is a much more complex thing than we ever understood before. So there's a lot for us to learn about theory, knowledge, and study.

How do we transform education to create a more participatory democracy? Representative democracy emerged a couple hundred years ago with the nation-state. We're now in the period when there are a lot of questions about the nation-state. What is the nation-state? What is its relationship to the world? And we have a version of democracy, which is obviously dysfunctional in Washington and elsewhere in the world. So we are challenged to create another democracy, and I believe it can begin on the school level. We can start at kindergarten to involve parents and teachers and children in this other education that is possible. The role that labor played in building the movements of the Thirties is now being played by the people involved in education. And that involves parents, teachers, and children because education is the creation of human beings. What's important to us today is not the manufacture of things as much as it is the creation of people.

iw: I'd like to pick up on how after Seattle came the World Social Forum. There's something very different about the World Social Forum from all previous attempts at changing the world. Up to 1968 all the major antisystemic movements—whether they were Communists or Social Democrats in the countries where they were strong or the national liberation movements—were all hierarchical organizations. Each believed they should be the only organization in the country, and that all other kinds of organizations had to be subordinated segments of them. If there was a women's group, it should be a women's group of the labor movement or of the Communist Party or of the national liberation movement. If there was a youth group, an ecology group, or a peace group, all of them had to be part of the one—the single movement which was hierarchical and stood for "the Revolution" because after "the Revolution" everything would be better.

What 1968 did all over the place was end this sense of the single hierarchical movement as the only movement. And we fiddled around with a lot of alternative possibilities; I won't go through them all. But finally after thirty or forty years we came up with the World Social Forum.

What is the World Social Forum? The World Social Forum brings together movements—a whole range of movements from what might be considered just left of center reformist movements to wildly revolutionary movements and all kinds.

All kinds in terms of their scope—some are local, some are regional, some are national, some are international. And all kinds in terms of their focus—some of them are labor movements, some of them are women's movements, some of them are gay and lesbian movements, some of them are ecology movements. You name it; they show up at the World Social Forum.

And what does the World Social Forum say should happen? The first thing that should happen is that they should talk to each other and not denounce each other. And maybe by talking to each other, they'll begin to understand things that they didn't understand themselves in terms of their own movement and begin to understand the possibilities of cooperative political action on specific things or general things with these other movements.

I'm a great believer in the World Social Forum. I think it's been a remarkable success. People talk about how it hasn't been a success, how the world hasn't been transformed. Well, it isn't true that the world hasn't been transformed. The United States Social Forum didn't exist in the 1990s. It wasn't even a thinkable possibility. And here it is, we're in the second one. And there are European Social Forums and Asian Social Forums and African Social Forums and regional Social Forums and thematic Social Forums. It's a "growth industry."

Laughs from audience.

And they're different, and they argue. People are unhappy about this and unhappy about that, and at least at the level of the World Social Forum, they've been tinkering with the way they've been run. At each meeting they're a little bit different because of the criticism of how it was run in the previous meeting, and we've been improving the process.

Now there are some people who say "yeah, but where's the action?" Well, the action is where we make the action. It isn't in the *meeting* of the World Social Forum or in the *meeting* of the United States Social Forum. But there is action, and a lot of that action is the consequence of the networking that was made possible by the Social Forum. So I think we've got a very strong mechanism here.

It isn't perfect. Who knows? Maybe five years from now they won't exist anymore, and we'll replace them with other things. I don't know. It's an uncertain world, and we're in an uncertain situation. We're feeling our way all the time, but we build on the positive and so far this meeting has been positive. The World Social Forum has been positive. I hope some of you are going to be able to get to the Dakar meeting in 2011. It's the second one in Africa. It's an important one, and I think we're going to be able to move forward from there.

GLB: You know Immanuel was at Porto Alegre; he was at Mumbai and I don't know how many other Social Forums. I haven't been to them, but we're so fortunate that he's here for our Social Forum in Detroit. The U.S. Social Forum is a process. They're trying to learn from each one to go to the next.

SK: Grace, I wanted you to address two issues. First, socialism is back in the news these days not only because the economic crisis is opening people's eyes to alternatives to capitalism but also because right-wing critics are denouncing Obama as a "socialist." What does socialism mean to you today? Second, I'd like you to respond to Immanuel's last point about changing concepts of revolution. You've written about how we have to see revolution not just as a one-time event that solves everything but as a protracted process—that everything we do is about creating the new relations that go into social transformation. So could you speak more about what is most important about new concepts of revolution?

GLB: I'm interested in the question "What is socialism?" I think we need to ask ourselves where the concept of socialism came from. We need to understand how the utopian socialism of the early nineteenth century was replaced by the scientific socialism of Marx and Engels and how Marx saw socialism as part of a sequence toward communism. He saw socialism as the stage at which workers took power in order to deal with the distribution of goods in a different way than the capitalist model. And if you're not a socialist, you're a knave. If you don't believe that we should have more *human* relationships among ourselves, you're a knave.

But if you're still a socialist, you're a fool. Because you're not thinking historically enough. You're not recognizing that the world we're living in is not the world of Karl Marx—that Marx was born in 1818, that he grew up in nineteenth-century Europe where there was a great deal of scarcity, so he was naturally and humanly concerned with economic growth. But we're not living in the nineteenth century. So we can't use the same words with the same sort of naïveté that we tend to do. Every concept has a historical origin. It's born at a particular time out of the creativity of intellectuals and people. And we have to create our own views of the revolutionary change that's required. What we know is that it's not going to be hierarchical in the way that it has been in the past. We know that it's not going to be patriarchal in the way that it has been in the past. We know that it's not going to involve the same industrialization and lack of contact with the Earth as it has in the past. We know a lot of fundamental things about it. And we have to find out how to recreate those fundamentals in practice and theory.

Most people still have in their minds the sort of hierarchical concept of revolution that came out of the insurrection of 1917. They haven't thought enough about what's happened since 1917—how those who capture state power become prisoners of the state. I think that as radicals we haven't discussed seriously enough or internalized the changing concepts of revolution. I'm sure a lot of you know [the late Italian Marxist] Antonio Gramsci and know how he said that we have "wars of movement" and "wars of position." We are in a period where we need to see ourselves not as capturing the state but as developing new ideas that will replace the ideas of the system. Because the ruling class rules

not only through force, as Gramsci would say, but through its
cultural hegemony.

So as intellectuals we have a really serious challenge.
How do we create the new ideas that are necessary? How do
we create alternatives? How do we get beyond oppositional
thinking and all the anger that is involved in oppositional
thinking, which really bogs us down? And how do we really
understand that revolution is a new beginning? It's not a
new beginning only in terms of economic systems and how
we make our living, but it's also a new beginning in how we
think and how we become more human. Each revolution is an
advance in our concept of what it means to be human.

Back in 1917 they couldn't help thinking in a hierarchical
way. In the White House they can't help thinking in a
hierarchical way. The only way they can solve the education
crisis is to have more testing and more punishment. They're
not able to think about another way of education that will
make us all more participants in creating our world and in
governing our world. So all these are enormous challenges that
we face. And I think if we come out of this U.S. Social Forum
with one thing, we should feel enormously challenged to
become more theoretical as well as more practical,
more imaginative.

IW: The world that I want and the world we should want is a
world that is relatively democratic and relatively egalitarian.
That's not the kind of world we have now. That's not the kind
of world we have ever had. What institutions will maintain a
world that is relatively democratic and relatively egalitarian?
I don't think we know. I often say that if people were sitting
around in the late fifteenth century and saying, "Oh goodness,
feudalism is coming to an end, and it's going to be replaced by
capitalism. What kinds of structures will this capitalist system
have?," how many of them could have in 1450 imagined the
kinds of structures which over five hundred years were developed in the capitalist world-economy in order to maintain the

system and allow it to function and allow it to meet its objectives?

So I don't think we can sit around and say that in the twenty-second century, in the twenty-third century there's going to be structures of the following kind which we can give a name to—we can call it socialist, we can call it anything we want—that will fulfill this need. What we can say is we've got to set it up on a certain fundamental thrust. And that thrust is to say we want a system that's relatively democratic and relatively egalitarian. I use the word "relatively" because it's never going to be perfect. There ain't no such thing, but we can do a lot better than we have done historically in the capitalist world-system. I don't think we have a single democratic country in the world, and I don't think that we ever have. We certainly haven't had any egalitarian countries in the world, including those that call themselves socialist. Creating one will be hard and something very new, so we've got to push in the right direction. We can't do more in the year 2010 than push in the right direction. And it's vain to think we can.

Is Venezuela establishing twenty-first century socialism? I don't believe that. I don't believe they can—even with the best will in the world—within Venezuela create twenty-first century socialism. Are they doing things that push in the right direction? Yes, for the moment, but we have to evaluate that as we have to evaluate everywhere, in every way. But push we can. So when workers in China push for a better deal, that's a good thing—just as it is a good thing if they do it in Detroit. It's pushing in the right direction, and I don't care what the name of the government is.

GLB: I just want to say I think it's wonderful to be in a room where people talk about the *nineteenth* century and the *fifteenth* century. I think our society has lost that sense of connectedness. Such a wide gulf has emerged between the generations, and we don't realize how much of our humanity we've lost in that process. That's why I welcome this session so much.

SK *(reading question from the audience):* "What is your vision of the world of 2050?"

IW: In the year 2050, we'll talk of capitalism as a system of the past. But what is my vision? My vision is I don't know. You know, in chaos theory discussions, there's the concept of the butterfly flapping the wings. The butterfly flaps its wings over here, and at the other end of the world the climate changes in all sorts of ways because that's the impact of one butterfly flapping its wings. And I'd like to say *we're all butterflies.*

We're all flapping our wings every minute, not just once. Every minute it's a different situation, and we're flapping our wings and it depends how many people flap their wings in the right direction. So it's up to you. If enough of us flap our wings repeatedly, constantly pushing in the right direction, we might win out. It's fifty-fifty, but I think fifty-fifty is a lot, not a little.

But for God's sake, don't think that it's certain. It's not certain, not at all. And in 2050 you might be living in a miserable world. It depends on how many of us flap our wings in the right direction.

Big applause as audience members flap their arms like butterflies.

SK *(reading question from the audience):* "Can you two reflect on what keeps you going, motivated, and still struggling? What sustains you?" Young people want to know the answer to that question as they look forward to the struggle towards the world of 2050 that they will be making.

IW: What else can we possibly do?

GB: Well, I was very fortunate; I was born female. My mother did not know how to read and write because there were no schools for females in her little Chinese village. My father was very interested in education. I was a graduate student studying for my PhD, and I came across Hegel. And I discovered something I think we all need to learn—particularly in the United States—that progress does not take place like a shot out of a pistol. It takes the labor and suffering of the negative.

How to use the negative as a way to advance the positive is our challenge. We're not going to progress in a straight line. Linear progress is ridiculous, not real. The labor and suffering of the negative enriches our concept of what is possible.

So in these very difficult times I see so many fantastic things happening—people inventing new ways of cooperating. Artists and young people are coming to Detroit to live collectively because when you pursue individual success in our current system, you have to sell out too much of yourself. And if you want to challenge the system, you can't do that on your own.

But there are ways that you can take advantage of the economic stringencies to advance, to become more cooperative, and to live more collectively—to work together, to cook together, to eat together, and not buy a car for everybody in the house. You can bike, as I know many of you have done in order to get here. There are so many things that we can do that will make us more human and at the same time help to begin to create the new society. Because that's what we're all about, that's what our mission is.

I think we are not conscious of the degree to which our society has moved us to see people as "others," or how we've lost the essential quality that has allowed the human race to evolve. That sense that, as Gwendolyn Brooks put it, "we are each other's harvest; we are each other's business." It goes back to an epistemology, a theory of knowledge that is not just of the brain but of the heart. An epistemology of compassion that recognizes how we belong to each other, that recognizes we are each other's harvest, we are each other's business.

To be at that time on the clock of the universe when we can make that huge change from "othering" other people to feeling that they are part of us and we are part of them—that's a wonderful opportunity. It's a wonderful time to be alive.

AFTERWORD NOTE

Thanks to Sarah Coffey for providing an original transcription of this conversation.

INDEX

Text:	10.75/15 Janson MT Pro
Display:	Janson MT Pro
Compositor:	Toppan Best-set Premedia Limited
Indexer:	Ruth Elwell
Printer and Binder:	Maple Press Book Manufacturing Group